To Be Married

Other books by Wendi Momen

To Be Married

compiled by

Wendi Momen

*♡ With love,
To Noah + Bailey
- Mom -
July 2021*

George Ronald
Oxford

George Ronald, *Publisher*
www.grbooks.com

© Wendi Momen 2019
All Rights Reserved

A Cataloguing-in-Publication entry
is available from the British Library

ISBN 978-0-85398-624-9

Contents

For Moojan

My travelling companion

through all the worlds of God

Preface

. . . the institution of marriage as conceived and established by Bahá'u'lláh is extremely simple though of a vital social importance, constituting as it does the very foundation of social life.

From a letter written on behalf of Shoghi Effendi[1]

When relations within the family are conducted with due regard for justice, it will be an important factor in bringing about peace in the world.

Bahá'í International Community[2]

It is in recognition of the importance of marriage and families to communities, social life, the establishment of universal peace and the emergence of a new world civilization that this little book of verses from the holy scriptures, poets and thinkers is offered.

Acknowledgements

My heartfelt thanks

to Carolyn Wade, my long-time friend and colleague on the National Spiritual Assembly of the Bahá'ís of the United Kingdom, for sharing so many years of laughter and learning together and, more recently, a beautiful poem

and

to my friend and colleague at the Wilmette Institute (http://wilmetteinstitute.org/) Susanne Alexander of Marriage Transformation (https://marriagetransformation.com/) who has generously shared with me her own research, insights, knowledge and passion for making marriages strong and healthy

and

to the whole team at the Wilmette Institute who have made courses on marriage and family life accessible to people all over the world.

The publisher has made every effort to trace copyright owners. Where we have failed we offer our apologies and undertake to make proper acknowledgement in reprints.

Foreword

Travelling Companions
(A blog from 2008)

Their purpose must be this: to become loving companions and comrades and at one with each other for time and eternity.
'Abdu'l-Bahá, Bahá'í writings

Most of the journeys we make in this life are along familiar paths. We walk to school along the same pavements day after day. We drive to work along the same roads. We make our way to the same shops to buy our food and clothes.

When we leave these roads to go to a new place, we consider that we are embarking on an adventure, something challenging but also, perhaps, exciting and fun. We might take maps or sat navs if we do not know the new route at all; if we are going for a long time, we might pack suitcases with clothes and food. Occasionally we set out on an unknown path, not knowing exactly how to prepare for the journey or how long it will take or where it will end but knowing we will never return along that same route.

The road of our life is like this. We are embarked upon it before we know anything about it and we do not even get to choose our first travelling companions!

At some point, if we are lucky and we live in a society that allows choice, we may be able to choose a person to travel with. For Bahá'ís this is a free choice and then, to create the unity necessary for the journey to proceed without a hitch, all the parents must agree.

Bahá'ís know that choosing a travelling companion out of love and for his or her spiritual qualities, good character, moral behaviour and ability to live a practical life with high ethical principles – as well as being attracted to his or her appearance and sense of humour! – is central to whether the journey will be pleasant or a misery.

The other side of this is being all these things oneself!

Having found a travelling companion, we then set out on this unknown path. There is a general map across the terrain and some guideposts as well as lots of advice from people who have set out – successfully or unsuccessfully – on a similar route. Knowing which map to trust is key! But in fact the road is a completely new one that no one has trod before and it is necessary for us to find our own way along it.

It helps to know how to read the general map, of

course, and to follow the guideposts where they exist. Bahá'ís, for example, use the map provided by the Bahá'í writings which shows that the way forward is a path of service to humanity linked to a love of God and adherence to His laws.

Many of the guidelines for a safe journey are found in the Bahá'í writings: love, justice, equality, non-violence, consultation, respect, trustworthiness. There is a section on crossing the badlands: love, consultation, faith, consultation, hope, consultation, perseverance, consultation, patience, consultation, more love, consultation . . .

Many travellers on this journey are joined at some point by younger travellers they have to guide along the path for some way. Interestingly, in this connection the guidelines contain a big section on mining – for gems – and another on sustainability and yet another on building bridges.

As they travel the companions may well discover they can improve the condition of the road if each works to create the conditions and environment in which the other can do his or her best work.

The guidelines acknowledge that while it may seem that most of the journey is uphill, this is better than going downhill. These Bahá'í guidelines also point out that if the travelling companions walk hand in hand along the road – admittedly they sometimes have to drag each other along it – then their unity will make walking easier.

An unusual characteristic of this particular journey is that the farther the companions travel together, the more energy they get, probably because their relationship is a 'gleaming out of the love of God'.

As they go along, the path becomes wider but they get closer and closer together so that sometimes it appears as if they are just one person. When this happens, they are 'aglow with the same wine, both are enamoured of the same matchless Face, both live and move through the same spirit, both are illumined by the same glory'. Because the bond between them is a physical and a spiritual one, 'it is a bond that will abide forever'.

So far, as of today, I have been walking this uphill path with my husband for 37 years.*

As I write, he is in Israel and I am in Italy but somehow we are closer than ever and the road seems to stretch ahead of us forever.

Wendi Momen
* It is 48 years now

Meaning and Purpose of Marriage

Bahá'í marriage is the commitment of the two parties one to the other, and their mutual attachment of mind and heart. Each must, however, exercise the utmost care to become thoroughly acquainted with the character of the other, that the binding covenant between them may be a tie that will endure forever. Their purpose must be this: to become loving companions and comrades and at one with each other for time and eternity . . .

The true marriage of Bahá'ís is this, that husband and wife should be united both physically and spiritually, that they may ever improve the spiritual life of each other, and may enjoy everlasting unity throughout all the worlds of God. This is Bahá'í marriage.

'Abdu'l-Bahá[1]

Marriage is an act of will that signifies and involves a mutual gift, which unites the spouses and binds them to their eventual souls, with whom they make up a sole family – a domestic church.

Pope John Paul II

O ye my two beloved children! The news of your union, as soon as it reached me, imparted infinite joy and gratitude. Praise be to God, those two faithful birds have sought shelter in one nest. I beseech God that He may enable them to raise an honoured family, for the importance of marriage lieth in the bringing up of a richly blessed family, so that with entire gladness they may, even as candles, illuminate the world. For the enlightenment of the world dependeth upon the existence of man. If man did not exist in this world, it would have been like a tree without fruit. My hope is that you both may become even as one tree, and may, through the outpourings of the cloud of loving-kindness, acquire freshness and charm, and may blossom and yield fruit, so that your line may eternally endure.

Upon ye be the Glory of the Most Glorious.

'Abdu'l-Bahá[2]

. . . whereas Bahá'u'lláh has not made marriage a binding obligation, He has nevertheless attributed to it such spiritual and social significance as no individual believer, under normal circumstances, can well be justified in disregarding it. In fact, in His Book of Laws (the 'Kitáb-i-Aqdas') He emphatically stresses its importance, and defines its essential purpose, namely the procreation of children and their training in the Religion of God, that they may know and adore Him, and mention and praise His Name.

From a letter written on behalf of Shoghi Effendi[3]

The Bahá'í Teachings do not only encourage marital life, considering it the natural and normal way of existence for every sane, healthy and socially-conscious and responsible person, but raise marriage to the status of a Divine institution, its chief and sacred purpose being the perpetuation of the human race – which is the very flower of the entire creation – and its elevation to the true station destined for it by God.

From a letter written on behalf of Shoghi Effendi[4]

. . . the fundamental purpose of marriage is to bring other souls into this world, to serve God and love Him.

Shoghi Effendi[5]

. . . the very purpose of marriage is the procreation of children who, when grown up, will be able to know God and to recognize and observe His Command-ments and Laws as revealed through His Messengers. Marriage is thus, according to the Bahá'í Teachings, primarily a social and moral act. It has a purpose which transcends the immediate personal needs and interests of the parties . . .

From a letter written on behalf of Shoghi Effendi[6]

Then God said, 'Let us make humankind in our image, according to our likeness; and let them have dominion over the fish of the sea, and over the birds of the air, and over the cattle, and over all the wild animals of the earth, and over every creeping thing that creeps upon the earth.'

So God created humankind in his image, in the image of God he created them; male and female he created them.

God blessed them, and God said to them, 'Be fruitful and multiply, and fill the earth and subdue it; and have dominion over the fish of the sea and over the birds of the air and over every living thing that moves upon the earth.'

Genesis 1:26–8

A relationship is not meant to be the joining at the hip of two emotional invalids. The purpose of a relationship is not for two incomplete people to become one, but rather, for two complete people to join together for the greater glory of God.

Relationships are part of a vast plan for our enlightenment, the Holy Spirit's blueprint by which each individual Soul is led to greater awareness and expanded love. Relationships are the Holy Spirit's laboratories in which He brings together people who have the maximal opportunity for mutual growth.

Marianne Williamson

Marriage is the intimate union and equal partnership of a man and a woman. It comes to us from the hand of God, who created male and female in his image, so that they might become one body and might be fertile and multiply. Though man and woman are equal as God's children, they are created with important differences that allow them to give themselves and to receive the other as a gift.

For Your Marriage[7]

Praise God who has created courtship and marriage, joy and gladness, feasting and laughter, pleasure and delight, love, brotherhood, peace and fellowship.

The Methodist Service Book

Like fingerprints, all marriages are different.

George Bernard Shaw

Sanctity of Marriage

. . . marriage is a very serious and sacred relationship.
From a letter written on behalf of Shoghi Effendi[1]

Marriage is an ethnic weaving together of families, of two Souls with their individual fates and destinies, of time and eternity. Everyday life married to the timeless mysteries of the Soul.

Thomas Moore

Marriage is, in the 'Aqdas', set forth as a most sacred and binding tie.
From a letter written on behalf of Shoghi Effendi[2]

One should believe in marriage as in the immortality of the Soul.

Honore de Balzac

Bahá'u'lláh considers the marriage bond very sacred
. . .
From a letter written on behalf of Shoghi Effendi[3]

Bahá'u'lláh has laid great emphasis on the sanctity of marriage, and the believers should exert their utmost to create harmony in their homes . . .
From a letter written on behalf of Shoghi Effendi[4]

Bahá'ís should be profoundly aware of the sanctity of marriage and should strive to make their marriages an eternal bond of unity and harmony. This requires effort and sacrifice and wisdom and self-abnegation.
From a letter written on behalf of the Universal House of Justice[5]

Love is the most ecstatic intensive consciousness of the cosmic forces of the Universe. This is why in all religions, marriage is a sacrament, a Divine Phenomenon.

Robert Muller

Love

The Nature of Love

Love is the very cause of life . . .
'Abdu'l-Bahá[1]

Love is a taste of paradise.
Sholem Aleichem

The very flower of the spirit of man is his capacity for love.
Rúḥíyyih Khánum[2]

Love alone is capable of uniting living beings in such a way as to complete and fulfil them, for it alone takes them and joins them with what is deepest in themselves.
Pierre Teilhard de Chardin

When someone loves you, the way they say your name is different. You know that your name is safe in their mouth.
Billy, age 4

Where there is love there is no darkness.

Burundi proverb

Love is my foundation
Wisdom is my capital
Struggle is my manner
Truth is my redeemer
Sorrow is my companion
Love is my foundation

Jimmy Cliff

What a power is love! It is the most wonderful, the greatest of all living powers.

Love gives life to the lifeless. Love lights a flame in the heart that is cold. Love brings hope to the hopeless and gladdens the hearts of the sorrowful.

In the world of existence there is indeed no greater power than the power of love. When the heart of man is aglow with the flame of love, he is ready to sacrifice all – even his life. In the Gospel it is said God is love.

There are four kinds of love. The first is the love that flows from God to man; it consists of the inexhaustible graces, the Divine effulgence and heavenly illumination. Through this love the world of being receives life. Through this love man is endowed with physical existence, until, through the breath of the

Holy Spirit – this same love – he receives eternal life and becomes the image of the Living God. This love is the origin of all the love in the world of creation.

The second is the love that flows from man to God. This is faith, attraction to the Divine, enkindlement, progress, entrance into the Kingdom of God, receiving the Bounties of God, illumination with the lights of the Kingdom. This love is the origin of all philanthropy; this love causes the hearts of men to reflect the rays of the Sun of Reality.

The third is the love of God towards the Self or Identity of God. This is the transfiguration of His Beauty, the reflection of Himself in the mirror of His Creation. This is the reality of love, the Ancient Love, the Eternal Love. Through one ray of this Love all other love exists.

The fourth is the love of man for man. The love which exists between the hearts of believers is prompted by the ideal of the unity of spirits. This love is attained through the knowledge of God, so that men see the Divine Love reflected in the heart. Each sees in the other the Beauty of God reflected in the soul, and finding this point of similarity, they are attracted to one another in love. This love will make all men the waves of one sea, this love will make them all the stars of one heaven and the fruits of one tree. This love will bring the realization of true accord, the foundation of real unity . . .

These four kinds of love originate from God.

These are rays from the Sun of Reality; these are the Breathings of the Holy Spirit; these are the Signs of the Reality.

'Abdu'l-Bahá[3]

Love, A Spiritual Attribute

Where there is love, nothing is too much trouble, and there is always time.

Attributed to 'Abdu'l-Bahá

He who is filled with love is filled with God himself.

St Augustine of Hippo

O Perfect Love

O perfect Love, all human thought transcending,
Lowly we kneel in prayer before thy throne
That theirs may be the love which knows no ending,
Whom thou for evermore dost join in one.

O perfect Life, be thou their full assurance
Of tender charity and steadfast faith,
O patient hope, and quiet brave endurance,
With childlike trust that fears not pain nor death.

Grant them the joy which brightens earthly sorrow,
Grant them the peace which calms all earthly strife;
And to life's day the glorious unknown morrow
That dawns upon eternal love and life.

Dorothy Frances Gurney

There are two kinds of love. Our love. God's love.
But God makes both kinds of them.

Jenny, age 4

Love is a Great Thing

Love is a great thing, yea, a great and thorough good.
By itself it makes what is heavy light; and it bears
even.

For it carries a burden which is no burden; and
makes everything that is bitter, sweet and tasteful . . .

Love desires to be aloft, and will not be kept back
by anything low and mean.

Love desires to be free, and estranged from all
worldly affections, and not to be entangled by any
outward prosperity, or by any adversity subdued.

Nothing is sweeter than love, nothing more cou-
rageous, nothing higher, nothing wider, nothing
more pleasant, nothing fuller nor better in heaven or
earth: because it is born of God, and cannot rest but
in God, above all created things . . .

Love feels no burden, thinks nothing of trouble,

attempts what is above its strength, pleads no excuse of impossibility. It is therefore able to undertake all things, and it completes many things, and warrants them to take effect, where he who does not love would faint and lie down . . .

Love is active and sincere, courageous, patient, faithful, prudent and manly, and never seeking itself . . .

Love is circumspect, humble and upright; not yielding to softness or levity, nor attending to vain things; but sober, chaste, steady, quiet and guarded in all the senses.

Thomas a Kempis[4]

Love is our best friend, our helper, and the healer of the ills which prevent us from being happy.

Plato

Know thou of a certainty that Love is the secret of God's holy Dispensation, the manifestation of the All-Merciful, the fountain of spiritual outpourings. Love is heaven's kindly light, the Holy Spirit's eternal breath that vivifieth the human soul. Love is the cause of God's revelation unto man, the vital bond inherent, in accordance with the divine creation, in the realities of things. Love is the one means that ensureth true felicity both in this world and the next.

Love is the light that guideth in darkness, the living link that uniteth God with man, that assureth the progress of every illumined soul. Love is the most great law that ruleth this mighty and heavenly cycle, the unique power that bindeth together the divers elements of this material world, the supreme magnetic force that directeth the movements of the spheres in the celestial realms. Love revealeth with unfailing and limitless power the mysteries latent in the universe. Love is the spirit of life unto the adorned body of mankind, the establisher of true civilization in this mortal world, and the shedder of imperishable glory upon every high-aiming race and nation.

O ye beloved of the Lord! Strive to become the manifestations of the love of God, the lamps of divine guidance shining amongst the kindreds of the earth with the light of love and concord.

'Abdu'l-Bahá[5]

Though I speak with the tongues of men and of angels, but have not love I am only a resounding gong or clanging cymbal. And though I have the gift of prophecy, and can understand all mysteries and all knowledge, and though I have faith, that can move mountains, but have not love, I am nothing. And though I give all I possess to the poor, and surrender my body to the flames, but have not love, I gain nothing.

Love suffers long and is kind; love does not envy; love does not parade itself, is not puffed up; does not behave rudely, does not seek its own, is not provoked, thinks no evil; does not rejoice in iniquity, but rejoices in the truth; bears all things, believes all things, hopes all things, endures all things.

Love never fails. But whether there are prophecies, they will fail; whether there are tongues, they will cease; whether there is knowledge, it will vanish away. For we know in part and we prophesy in part. But when that which is perfect has come, then that which is in part will be done away.

When I was a child, I spoke as a child, I understood as a child, I thought as a child; but when I became a man, I put away childish things. For now we see in a mirror, darkly, but then face to face. Now I know in part, but then I shall know just as I also am known.

And now abide faith, hope, love, these three; but the greatest of these is love.

1 Corinthians 13:1–13 (NKJV)

Falling in Love

Love is friendship caught fire;
it is quiet, mutual confidence, sharing and forgiving.
It is loyalty through good and bad times.

It settles for less than perfection,
    and makes allowances for human weaknesses.
Love is content with the present,
        hopes for the future,
    and does not brood over the past.
It is the day-in and day-out chronicles
        of irritations, problems, compromises, small
            disappointments,
        big victories, and working toward common
            goals.
If you have love in your life, it can make up for a
    great many things you lack.
If you do not have it, no matter what else there is, it
    is not enough.

Laura Hendricks

Touched by an Angel
We, unaccustomed to courage
exiles from delight
live coiled in shells of loneliness
until love leaves its high holy temple
and comes into our sight
to liberate us into life.

Love arrives
and in its train come ecstasies
old memories of pleasure
ancient histories of pain.

Yet if we are bold,
love strikes away the chains of fear
from our souls.

We are weaned from our timidity
In the flush of love's light
we dare be brave

And suddenly we see
that love costs all we are
and will ever be.
Yet it is only love
which sets us free.

Maya Angelou

The Madness of Love

Love accepteth no existence and wisheth no life:
In death it seeth life, and in shame it seeketh glory.
To merit the madness of love, one must abound in
sanity; to merit the bonds of the Friend, one must be
free in spirit. Blessed the neck that is caught in His
noose, and happy the head that falleth on the dust in
the path of His love. Wherefore, O friend, renounce
thy self, that thou mayest find the Peerless One; and
soar beyond this mortal world, that thou mayest find
thy nest in the abode of heaven. Be as naught, if thou

wouldst kindle the fire of being and be fit for the pathway of love.

Bahá'u'lláh[6]

Love setteth a world aflame at every turn and layeth waste every land wherein it raiseth its banner. Being hath no existence in its kingdom; the wise wield no command within its realm. The leviathan of love swalloweth the master of reason and slayeth the lord of knowledge. It drinketh the seven seas, but its heart's thirst is still unquenched and it asketh, 'Is there yet any more?' It shunneth its own self and draweth away from all on earth.

Bahá'u'lláh[7]

A lover feareth nothing and can suffer no harm: Thou seest him chill in the fire and dry in the sea.

> A lover is he who is chill in hellfire;
> A knower is he who is dry in the sea.

Saná'í[8]

> Love's a stranger to earth and heaven too;
> In him are lunacies seventy and two.

Jalalu'd-Din Rumi[9]

It is related that one day they came upon Majnún
sifting the dust, his tears flowing down. They asked,
'What doest thou?' He said, 'I seek for Laylí.' 'Alas
for thee!' they cried, 'Laylí is of pure spirit, yet thou
seekest her in the dust!' He said, 'I seek her every-
where; haply somewhere I shall find her.'

Recounted by Bahá'u'lláh[10]

Love is a temporary madness, it erupts like volcanoes
and then subsides. And when it subsides you have to
make a decision. You have to work out whether your
root was so entwined together that it is inconceivable
that you should ever part. Because this is what love
is. Love is not breathlessness, it is not excitement, it is
not the promulgation of promises of eternal passion.
That is just being in love, which any fool can do.
Love itself is what is left over when being in love has
burned away, and this is both an art and a fortunate
accident. Those that truly love have roots that grow
towards each other underground, and when all the
pretty blossoms have fallen from their branches, they
find that they are one tree and not two.

Louis de Bernieres[11]

There was once a lover, it is said, who had sighed for
long years in separation from his beloved, and wasted
in the fire of remoteness. From the rule of love, his

breast was void of patience and his body weary of his spirit; he reckoned life without her as a mockery, and the world consumed him away. How many a day he found no respite from his longing; how many a night the pain of her kept him from sleep. His body was worn to a sigh, and his heart's wound had turned him to a cry of sorrow. A thousand lives would he freely have given for one taste of the cup of her presence, and yet even this was not within his reach. The doctors knew no cure for him, and companions avoided his company; yea, physicians have no remedy for one sick of love, unless the favour of the beloved deliver him.

At last the tree of his longing yielded the fruit of despair, and the fire of his hope fell to ashes. Then one night he could bear life no more, and he left his house for the marketplace. On a sudden, a watchman followed after him. He broke into a run, with the watchman in swift pursuit; then other watchmen came together and barred every passage to the weary one. And that wretched one cried from his heart, and ran here and there, and moaned to himself, 'Surely this watchman is 'Izrá'íl, my angel of death, following so fast upon me, or he is a tyrant of men, prompted by hatred and malice.' His feet carried him on – that hapless one bleeding with the arrow of love – while his heart lamented. Then he came to a garden wall, and with untold pain and trouble he scaled it. He saw that it was very high; yet, forgetting his life, he threw himself down into the garden.

And there he beheld his beloved with a lamp in her hand, searching for a ring she had lost.

When the heart-surrendered lover looked upon his ravishing love, he drew a great breath and lifted his hands in prayer, crying, 'O God! Bestow honour upon the watchman, and riches and long life. For the watchman was Gabriel, guiding this poor one; or he was Isráfíl, bringing life to this wretched one!'

Indeed, his words were true; for he had found many a secret justice in this seeming tyranny of the watchman, and had seen how many a mercy lay hid behind the veil. In one stroke of wrath, the guard had joined one who was athirst in the desert of love to the sea of the beloved, and dispelled the darkness of separation with the shining light of reunion. He had led one who was afar to the garden of nearness, and guided an ailing soul to the heart's physician.

Now if the lover could have seen the end, he would from the beginning have blessed the watchman, prayed God on his behalf, and seen his tyranny as justice; but since the end was veiled to him, he lamented and made his plaint in the beginning. Yet those who journey in the garden land of true knowledge, since they see the end in the beginning, behold peace in war and conciliation in enmity.

Bahá'u'lláh[12]

When in love, a cliff becomes a meadow.
Ethiopian proverb

Learning to Love, Being Loved, Loving

We can only learn to love by loving.
Iris Murdoch

To be loved but not known is comforting but super-ficial. To be known and not loved is our greatest fear. But to be fully known and truly loved is, well, a lot like being loved by God. It is what we need more than anything. It liberates us from pretence, humbles us out of our self-righteousness, and fortifies us for any difficulty life can throw at us.
Timothy Keller[13]

Our love is like the misty rain that falls softly but floods the river.
African proverb

Love is Blind

Love recognizes no barriers. It jumps hurdles, leaps fences, penetrates walls to arrive at its destination full of hope.
Maya Angelou

Love is blind
Doesn't recognize gender
Is given to egotists
and misogynists, alike
Is introduced to the plain
and old and the maimed,
An indiscriminate visitor
To the reluctant
the dying.
Flows to the realms of
Four-footed creatures,
Under their feet
The growing things get it,
Down to the dust its strokes the land
Up to the stars it puts its hand
Love is blind.

J.M. Wells[14]

Love has to be shown by deeds, not words.
Swahili proverb

Love shall come to complete you; first know, then be yourself.
From 'Knobeco and Love', an African folktale

You can give without loving, but you can never love without giving. The great acts of love are done by those who are habitually performing small acts of kindness. We pardon to the extent that we love. Love is knowing that even when you are alone, you will never be lonely again. And great happiness of life is the conviction that we are loved. Loved for ourselves. And even loved in spite of ourselves.

Victor Hugo[15]

Beloved, let us love one another: for love is of God; and every one that loveth is born of God, and knoweth God. He that loveth not knoweth not God; for God is love. In this was manifested the love of God toward us . . .

Beloved, if God so loved us, we ought also to love one another. No man hath seen God at any time. If we love one another, God dwelleth in us, and his love is perfected in us.

1 John 4:7–12

Love and kindness are never wasted. They always make a difference. They bless the one who receives them, and they bless you, the giver.

Barbara De Angelis

Love holds me captive again
and I tremble with bittersweet longing

As a gale on the mountainside bends the oak tree
I am rocked by my love
You are sweet, O Love, dear Love,
You are soft as the nesting dove.
Come to my heart and bring it rest
As the bird flies home to its welcome nest.

Sappho

Love seeketh not itself to please,
Nor for itself hath any care,
But for another gives its ease,
And builds a Heaven in Hell's despair.

William Blake

Love is a force more formidable than any other. It
is invisible – it cannot be seen or measured, yet it
is powerful enough to transform you in a moment,
and offer you more joy than any material possession
could.

Barbara De Angelis

True Love is but a humble,
low-born thing,
And hath its food served up
in earthen ware;
It is a thing to walk with,
hand in hand,
Through the everydayness of this
workday world.

J.M. Lowell

The Path to Marriage

Finding the Right Person

The minute I heard my first love story I started looking for you, not knowing how blind that was.

Lovers don't finally meet somewhere. They're in each other all along.

Rumi

Marriage is not the ritual or an end, it is a long, intricate, intimate dance together and nothing matters more than your own sense of balance and choice of partner.

Amy Bloom

The secret of a happy marriage is finding the right person. You know they're right if you love to be with them all the time.

Julia Child

Identifying Character

Bahá'í marriage is union and cordial affection between the two parties. They must, however, exercise the utmost care and become acquainted with each other's character. This eternal bond should be made secure by a firm covenant, and the intention

should be to foster harmony, fellowship and unity
and to attain everlasting life.

'Abdu'l-Bahá[1]

. . . clothe yourselves with compassion, kindness,
humility, gentleness and patience. Bear with each
other and forgive one another if any of you has a
grievance against someone. Forgive as the Lord
forgave you. And over all these virtues put on love,
which binds them all together in perfect unity.

Colossians 3:12–14 (NIV)

Now that thou art returning to America thou must
think of taking unto thyself a wife. Do thou choose
a girl who may be suitable to thy intellectual and
spiritual ideals. She must be wise, intelligent, and
a symbol of aspiring perfection. She must take an
interest in all the problems pertaining to thy life, and
be thy companion and partner in every phase of thy
existence. She must be sympathetic, kind-hearted,
happy, and endowed with a joyful disposition. Then
thou must devote thyself to her happiness and love
her with a glorious, spiritual love.

Before choosing a wife a man must think soberly
and seriously that this girl will be his friend through-
out all his life. It is not a temporary matter. She is a
soul with whom he must associate all the days of his

life; she will be his mate and his intimate confidant; therefore, day by day their love and their attachment to each other must increase.

Attributed 'Abdu'l-Bahá[2]

There are qualities in everyone which we can appreciate and admire, and for which we can love them . . .
From a letter written on behalf of the Universal House of Justice[3]

A couple should study each other's character and spend time getting to know each other before they decide to marry, and when they do marry it should be with the intention of establishing an eternal bond.

The Universal House of Justice[4]

Why Love is Blind
I have heard of reasons manifold
Why Love must needs be blind;
But this the best of all I hold –
His eyes are in his mind,
What outward form and feature are
He guesseth but in part;
But what within is good and fair
He seeth with the heart.

S. T. Coleridge

'Chemistry'

Poem #63

Your hands in my hands, Happily meet
Your eyes and my eyes, Joyously greet
Your cheek 'gainst my cheek, Passingly sweet
Your lips to my lips, Rapture complete.

Joseph S. Cotter Jr.

You Came, Too

I came to the crowd seeking friends
I came to the crowd seeking love
I came to the crowd for understanding
I found you

I came to the crowd to weep
I came to the crowd to laugh
You dried my tears
You shared my happiness

I went from the crowd seeking you
I went from the crowd seeking me
I went from the crowd forever
You came, too

Nikki Giovanni

There is no teaching in the Bahá'í Faith that 'soul mates' exist. What is meant is that marriage should lead to a profound friendship of spirit, which will endure in the next world, where there is no sex, and no giving and taking in marriage; just the way we should establish with our parents, our children, our brothers and sisters and friends a deep spiritual bond which will be everlasting, and not merely physical bonds of human relationship.

Written on behalf of the Universal House of Justice[5]

Deciding to Marry

He realizes your desire to get married is quite a natural one, and he will pray that God will assist you to find a suitable companion with whom you can be truly happy and united in the service of the Faith. Bahá'u'lláh has urged marriage upon all people as the natural and rightful way of life. He has also, however, placed strong emphasis on its spiritual nature, which, while in no way precluding a normal physical life, is the most essential aspect of marriage. That two people should live their lives in love and harmony is of far greater importance than that they should be consumed with passion for each other. The one is a great rock of strength on which to lean in time of need; the other a purely temporary thing which may at any time die out.

From letter written on behalf of Shoghi Effendi[6]

I will make you brooches and toys for your delight
Of bird-song at morning and star-shine at night.
I will make a palace fit for you and me
Of green days in forests and blue days at sea.

I will make my kitchen, and you shall keep your
    room,
Where white flows the river and bright blows the
    broom,
And you shall wash your linen and keep your body
    white
In rainfall at morning and dewfall at night.

And this shall be for music when no one else is near,
The fine song for singing, the rare song to hear!
That only I remember, that only you admire,
Of the broad road that stretches and the roadside
    fire.

Robert Louis Stevenson[7]

You require but a simple 'Yes'? Such a small word –
but such an important one. But should not a heart so
full of unutterable love as mine utter this little word
with all its might? I do so and my innermost soul
whispers always to you.

Clara Wieck

I wish to assure you, in particular, of his supplications for your guidance in connection with your proposed plan to unite in marriage . . . May the Beloved help you in forming the right decision, and spare you the anxiety and suffering which too hasty action in such matters inevitably produces. You should give this question, which is of such vital concern to your future, the full consideration it deserves, and examine all its aspects carefully and dispassionately. The final decision rests with you and . . . [the proposed partner].

From a letter written on behalf of Shoghi Effendi [8]

Engagement

I knew it was love, and I felt it was glory.
Lord Byron

. . . a man shall leave his father and mother and be
joined to his wife, and they shall become one flesh.
Genesis 2:24

My beloved speaks and says to me:
 'Arise, my love, my fair one,
and come away;
for now the winter is past,
the rain is over and gone.
The flowers appear on the earth;
the time of singing has come,
and the voice of the turtle dove
is heard in our land.
The fig tree puts forth its figs,
and the vines are in blossom;
they give forth fragrance.
Arise, my love, my fair one,
and come away.'
Song of Solomon 2:10–13

When you love someone, you love him as he is.
Charles Péguy

Long as I live, my heart will never vary
For no one else, however fair or good,
Brave, resolute or rich, of gentle blood,
My choice is made, and I will have no other.

French poem

As for the question regarding marriage under the Law of God: first thou must choose one who is pleasing to thee, and then the matter is subject to the consent of father and mother. Before thou makest thy choice, they have no right to interfere.

'Abdu'l-Bahá[1]

. . . the consent of all living parents is required for a Bahá'í marriage . . . This great law He has laid down to strengthen the social fabric, to knit closer the ties of the home, to place a certain gratitude and respect in the hearts of children for those who have given them life and sent their souls out on the eternal journey toward their Creator.

From a letter written on behalf of Shoghi Effendi[2]

Bahá'í marriage is the commitment of the two parties one to the other, and their mutual attachment of mind and heart.

'Abdu'l-Bahá[3]

Thou art my life, my love, my heart, the very eyes of me, And hast command of every part to live and die for thee.

Robert Herrick

I know not if I know what true love is,
But if I know, then, if I love not him,
I know there is none other I can love.

Alfred, Lord Tennyson

Love is born with the pleasure of looking at each other, it is fed with the necessity of seeing each other, it is concluded with the impossibility of separation!

José Martí

Love is, after all, the gift of oneself.

Jean Anouilh

Understand, I'll skip quietly away from the noisy crowd when I see the pale stars rising, blooming, over the oaks. I'll pursue solitary pathways through the pale twilit meadows with only this one dream: You come too.

R.M. Rilke

This principle [of the equality of women and men] is far more than the enunciation of admirable ideals; it has profound implications in all aspects of human relations and must be an integral element of Bahá'í domestic and community life. The application of this principle gives rise to changes in habits and practices which have prevailed for many centuries. An example of this is found in the response provided on behalf of Shoghi Effendi to a question whether the traditional practice whereby the man proposes marriage to the woman is altered by the Bahá'í Teachings to permit the woman to issue a marriage proposal to the man; the response is, '[Shoghi Effendi] . . . wishes to state that there is absolute equality between the two, and that no distinction of preference is permitted . . .'

From a letter of Universal House of Justice[4]

The Bahá'í youth . . . should be advised, nay even encouraged, to contract marriage while still young and in full possession of their physical vigour. Economic factors, no doubt, are often a serious hindrance to early marriage, but in most cases are only an excuse, and as such should not be overstressed.

From a letter written on behalf of Shoghi Effendi[5]

The Wedding

Wedding Day

Marriage is a holy institution and much encouraged in this blessed cause. Now you two are no longer two, but one. Bahá'u'lláh's wish is that all men be of one mind and consider themselves of one great household, that the mind of mankind be not divided against itself.

It is my wish and hope that you may be blessed in your life. May God help you to render great service to the kingdom of Abhá and may you become a means of its advancement.

May joy be increased to you as the years go by, and may you become thriving trees bearing delicious and fragrant fruits which are the blessings in the path of service.

Words attributed to 'Abdu'l-Bahá at the marriage of
two Bahá'ís in London in 1911[1]

Make a joyful noise unto the Lord, all ye lands.
Serve the Lord with gladness: come before his
    presence with singing.
Know ye that the Lord he is God: it is he that hath
    made us, and not we ourselves; we are his people,
    and the sheep of his pasture.
Enter into his gates with thanksgiving, and into his
    courts with praise: be thankful unto him, and
    bless his name.

For the Lord is good; his mercy is everlasting; and his
truth endureth to all generations.

Psalms 100:1–5

. . . the union of created things doth ever yield most
laudable results. From the pairing of even the small-
est particles in the world of being are the grace and
bounty of God made manifest; and the higher the
degree, the more momentous is the union. 'Glory
be to Him Who hath created all the pairs, of such
things as earth produceth, and out of men them-
selves, and of things beyond their ken.' And above
all other unions is that between human beings, espe-
cially when it cometh to pass in the love of God.
Thus is the primal oneness made to appear; thus is
laid the foundation of love in the spirit. It is certain
that such a marriage as yours will cause the bestow-
als of God to be revealed. Wherefore do we offer
you felicitations and call down blessings upon you
and beg of the Blessed Beauty, through His aid and
favour, to make that wedding feast a joy to all and
adorn it with the harmony of Heaven.

'Abdu'l-Bahá[2]

The Wedding Day of Munírih Khánum and 'Abdu'l-Bahá

We continued to live in the house of Jináb-i Kalím for five months because of a lack of housing. Finally, Khájih 'Abbúd questioned Jináb-i Kalím about this matter and asked why the marriage had been delayed. Jináb-i Kalím did not give him a clear answer, until 'Abbúd himself realized that the problem was the lack of a room. Khájih 'Abbúd then opened a room from his own house, which adjoined the private quarters of the holy Household. He furnished the room with the utmost simplicity and purity, and then went to the Blessed Beauty to request Him to accept this room as he had prepared it for the Master. His request was accepted, and the night of union – preferable to a hundred thousand years – drew near.

On that night, I wore a white dress given to me by the Greatest Holy Leaf, and which was more precious than all the silks and brocades of paradise. At about three hours after sunset on that night of power, the life-giving voice of the incomparable Beloved could be heard from the Supreme Source. I was summoned to the presence of the Blessed Beauty, attended by Hadrat-i Khánum [Asíyih Khánum, the wife of Bahá'u'lláh].

The Ancient Beauty was seated under a mosquito net. He said, 'You have come! You are welcome!' Then He addressed me thus: 'O My Leaf and My

Handmaiden! Verily, we chose thee and accept thee to serve my Most Great Branch, and this is by my grace, which is not equalled by all the treasures of earth and heaven.' After bestowing numerous favours, He said, 'How many were the girls in Baghdad and Adrianople, and in this Most Great Prison who hoped to attain to this bounty, and whose hopes were not fulfilled. You must be thankful for this most great bestowal and great favour.' Then He dismissed me and bade me to withdraw 'under the protection of God'. After hearing these heavenly words and observing such divine bestowals, you can imagine how I felt and what a world was before my eyes.

> Said the heavens to the earth:
> 'If the Resurrection thou hast never seen,
> then behold!'

After that blessed and happy hour, I entered that sheltering paradise, immersed in worlds of ardent desire, attraction, effacement, and absolute nothingness. How blessed and exalted was that time! How joyous that hour in that room! There I observed the Most Great Branch in utmost grace, bounty, and majesty. Only God knows what happened at that time. After an hour or so, the Master's mother, the wife of Áqáy-i Kalím, the wife of the landlord, and their daughters all entered the room. The mother of Mírzá Muḥammad 'Alí had brought Tablets used especially for celebrating holy days and festive occasions. She handed me the Tablet that begins: 'The gates of paradise are opened and the celestial youth hath appeared' [Tablet of the Youth of Paradise] and told me to recite it. Without further ceremony, I took it and intoned it in a loud and melodious voice. From then on, whenever the wife of Khájih 'Abbúd saw me she would say: 'I shall never forget that night and that meeting; the sweetness of your voice still rings in my ears. No bride had ever chanted so at her own wedding!'

Munírih Khánum[3]

The Wedding Day of Rúḥíyyih Khánum and Shoghi Effendi

Surely the simplicity of the marriage of Shoghi Effendi – reminiscent of the simplicity of 'Abdu'l-Bahá's own marriage in the prison-city of 'Akká – should provide a thought-provoking example to the Bahá'ís everywhere. No one, with the exception of his parents, my parents and a brother and two sisters of his living in Haifa, knew it was to take place. He felt strongly urged to keep it a secret, knowing from past experience how much trouble any major event in the Cause invariably stirred up. It was therefore a stunning surprise to both the servants and the local Bahá'ís when his chauffeur drove him off, with me beside him, to visit the Holy Tomb of Bahá'u'lláh on the afternoon of March 25, 1937. His heart drew him to that Most Sacred Spot on earth at such a moment in his life. I remember I was dressed entirely in black for this unique occasion.

I wore a white lace blouse, but otherwise I was a typical example of the way oriental women dressed to go out into the streets in those days, the custom being to wear black. Although I was from the West Shoghi Effendi desired me to fit into the pattern of the life in his house – which was a very oriental one – as naturally and inconspicuously as possible and I was only too happy to comply with his wishes in every way. When we arrived at Bahjí and entered the Shrine he requested me to give him his ring, which I was wearing concealed about my neck, and this he placed on the ring-finger of my right hand, the same finger that corresponded to the one of his own on which he himself had always worn it. This was the only gesture he made. He entered the inner Shrine, beneath the floor of which Bahá'u'lláh is interred, and gathered up in a handkerchief all the dried petals and flowers that the keeper of the Shrine used to take from the threshold and place in a silver receptacle at the feet of Bahá'u'lláh. After he had chanted the Tablet of Visitation we came back to Haifa. There was no celebration, no flowers, no elaborate ceremony, no wedding dress, no reception. His mother and father, in compliance with the laws of Bahá'u'lláh, signified their consent by signing our marriage certificates and then I went back to the Western Pilgrim House across the street and joined my parents (who had not been present at any of these events), and Shoghi Effendi went to attend to his own affairs.

At dinnertime, quite as usual, the Guardian appeared, showering his love and congratulations on my mother and father. He took the handkerchief, full of such precious flowers, and with his inimitable smile gave them to my mother, saying he had brought them for her from the inner Shrine of Bahá'u'lláh.

My parents also signed the marriage certificate and after dinner and these events were over I walked home with Shoghi Effendi, my suitcases having been taken across the street by Fujita while we were at dinner. We visited for awhile with the Guardian's family and then went up to his two rooms which the Greatest Holy Leaf had had built for him so long ago.

The quietness, the simplicity, the reserve and dignity with which this marriage took place did not signify that the Guardian considered it an unimportant event – on the contrary. Over his mother's signature, but drafted by the Guardian, the following cable was sent to America:

ANNOUNCE ASSEMBLIES CELEBRATION MARRIAGE BELOVED GUARDIAN. INESTIMABLE HONOUR CONFERRED UPON HANDMAID OF BAHÁ'U'LLÁH

RÚḤÍYYIH KHÁNUM MISS MARY MAXWELL. UNION OF EAST AND WEST PROCLAIMED BY BAHÁ'Í FAITH CEMENTED. ZIAIYYIH MOTHER OF THE GUARDIAN.

A telegram similar to this was sent to Persia. This news, so long awaited, naturally produced great rejoicing amongst the Bahá'ís and messages flooded in to Shoghi Effendi from all parts of the world.

Rúḥíyyih Rabbaní[4]

The Wedding Vow
We will all, verily, abide by the Will of God.
Bahá'u'lláh[5]

A Marriage of Love

When, therefore, the people of Bahá undertake to marry, the union must be a true relationship, a spiritual coming together as well as a physical one, so that throughout every phase of life, and in all the worlds of God, their union will endure; for this real oneness is a gleaming out of the love of God.

'Abdu'l-Bahá[1]

That two people should live their lives in love and harmony is of far greater importance than that they should be consumed with passion for each other. The one is a great rock of strength on which to lean in time of need; the other a purely temporary thing which may at any time die out.

From a letter written on behalf of Shoghi Effendi[2]

Wherefore, wed Thou in the heaven of Thy mercy these two birds of the nest of Thy love, and make them the means of attracting perpetual grace; that from the union of these two seas of love a wave of tenderness may surge and cast the pearls of pure and goodly issue on the shore of life.

'Abdu'l-Bahá[3]

Love is often a fruit of marriage.

Moliere

If love and agreement are manifest in a single family, that family will advance, become illumined and spiritual.

'Abdu'l-Bahá[4]

Nourish continually the tree of your union with love and affection, so that it will remain ever green and verdant throughout all seasons and bring forth luscious fruits for the healing of nations . . .

Be like two sweet-singing birds perched upon the highest branches of the tree of life, filling the air with songs of love and rapture.

Lay the foundation of your affection in the very centre of your spiritual being, at the very heart of your consciousness, and let it not be shaken by adverse winds.

Attributed to 'Abdu'l-Bahá

The web of marriage is made by propinquity in the day to day living, side by side, looking outward and working in the same direction. It is woven in space and in time of the substance of life itself.

When the heart is flooded with love there is no room in it for fear, for doubt, for hesitation. And it is this lack of fear that makes for the dance. When each partner loves so completely that he has forgotten to ask himself whether he is loved in return; when he

only knows that he loves and is moving to music –
then, and then only, are two people able to dance
perfectly in time to the same rhythm.

Anne Morrow Lindbergh

There is no fear in love; but perfect love casteth out
fear . . .

1 John 4:18

I take in as my breath the sweet air that comes from
    you.
I witness your beauty every day.
I desire to hear your voice on the north wind each
    day
so the strength in my arms may be reborn with your
    love.
Call for me through eternity, and I will always be
    there.

Egyptian love poem

A successful marriage requires falling in love many
times . . . always with the same person.

Mignon McLaughlin

Never Marry But For Love

Never marry but for love; but see that thou lovest what is lovely. He that minds a body and not a soul has not the better part of that relationship, and will consequently lack the noblest comfort of a married life.

Between a man and his wife, nothing ought to rule but love. As love ought to bring them together, so it is the best way to keep them well together.

A husband and wife that love one another show their children that they should do so too. Others visibly lose their authority in their families by the contempt of one another, and teach their children to be unnatural by their own examples.

Let not enjoyment lessen, but augment, affection; it being the basest of passions to like when we have not, what we slight when we possess.

Here it is we ought to search out our pleasure, where the field is large and full of variety, and of an enduring nature; sickness, poverty or disgrace being not able to shake it because it is not under the moving influences of worldly contingencies.

Nothing can be more entire and without reserve; nothing more zealous, affectionate and sincere; nothing more contented than such a couple, nor greater temporal felicity than to be one of them.

William Penn

Appreciating One Another

To My Dear and Loving Husband

If ever two were one, then surely we.
If ever man were loved by wife, then thee;
If ever wife was happy in a man,
Compare with me, ye women, if you can.
I prize thy love more than whole mines of gold
Or all the riches that the East doth hold.
My love is such that rivers cannot quench,
Nor ought but love from thee give recompense.
Thy love is such I can no way repay.
The heavens reward thee manifold, I pray.
Then while we live, in love let's so persever[e]
That when we live no more, we may live ever.

Anne Bradstreet

Where there is no wife, there is no home.

Yugoslavian proverb

Happy is the man who finds a true friend, and far happier is he who finds that true friend in his wife.

Franz Schubert

A happy man married the women he loves.
A happier man loves the woman he marries.

African proverb

A good husband makes a good wife.

John Florio

My most brilliant achievement was my ability to be able to persuade my wife to marry me.

Winston Churchill

The most important thing a father can do for his children is to love their mother.

Rev Hesburgh

She brings the sunshine into the house; it is now a pleasure to be there.

Cecil Beaton

She who dwells with me whom I have loved with such communion, that no place on Earth can ever be solitude to me.

William Blake

A Marriage of Unity

... harmony, unity and love are ... the highest ideals in human relationships.
From a letter written on behalf of Shoghi Effendi[1]

Happy the bride and bridegroom and thrice happy are they whose love grows stronger day by day and whose union remains undissolved until the last day.
African-American blessing

If you want to go quickly, go alone.
If you want to go far, go together.
Anon.

A common vision can unite people of very different temperaments.
Timothy Keller[2]

The true basis of unity is service ...
From a letter written on behalf of Shoghi Effendi[3]

The greatest marriages are built on teamwork. A mutual respect, a healthy dose of admiration, and a never-ending portion of love and grace.
Fawn Weaver

Two souls with but a single thought
Two hearts that beat as one.

Maria Lovell

. . . the unity of your family should take priority over any other consideration. Bahá'u'lláh came to bring unity to the world, and a fundamental unity is that of the family.

From a letter written on behalf of the Universal House of Justice[4]

Well, what is a relationship? It's about two people having tremendous weaknesses and vulnerabilities, like we all do, and one person being able to strengthen the other in their areas of vulnerability, and vice versa. You need each other. You complete each other, passion and romance aside.

Jane Fonda

We find rest in those we love, and we provide a resting place in ourselves for those who love us.

St Bernard of Clairvaux

Neither man nor woman is perfect or complete without the other. Thus, no marriage or family, no ward or stake is likely to reach its full potential until husbands and wives, mothers and fathers, men and women work together in unity of purpose, respecting and relying upon each other's strengths.

Sheri L. Dew

The goal in marriage is not to think alike, but to think together.

Robert C. Dodds

What greater thing is there for two human Souls than to feel that they are joined . . . to beat one with each other in silent, unspeakable memories.

George Eliot

When two people are at one
in their inmost hearts,
they shatter even the strength
of iron or bronze.
And when two people understand each other
in their inmost hearts,
their words are sweet and strong,
like the fragrance of orchids.

I Ching

Chains do not hold a marriage together. It is threads, hundreds of tiny threads, which sew people together through the years.

Simone Signoret

I think long-lasting, healthy relationships are more important than the idea of marriage. At the root of every successful marriage is a strong partnership.

Carson Daly

. . . the joyful news of thy marriage to that luminous leaf hath been received, and hath infinitely gladdened the hearts of the people of God. With all humility, prayers of supplication have been offered at the Holy Threshold, that this marriage may be a harbinger of joy to the friends, that it may be a loving bond for all eternity, and yield everlasting benefits and fruits.

'Abdu'l-Bahá[5]

The Bahá'í approach to family unity combines elements of traditional wisdom with progressive principles and practical tools. Adherence to these teachings offers a bulwark against the forces of disintegration and a framework for the creation of strong, healthy, unified families.

The foundation and precondition for a Bahá'í

family is the loving relationship of husband and wife. Marriage, a divine creation, is intended to unite a couple 'both physically and spiritually, that they may ever improve the spiritual life of each other'. A man and woman, having freely chosen one another and having obtained the consent of their parents, marry, according to Bahá'í law, in the presence of witnesses designated by the elected governing council of the community, the Local Spiritual Assembly. With the words 'We will all, verily, abide by the will of God', recited by both bride and groom, the two commit themselves to God and, thereby, to one another.

One purpose of marriage is the creation of a new generation who will love God and serve humanity. The task of the family is, therefore, to establish a loving, respectful and harmonious relationship among parents and children.

Harmony and cooperation in the family, as in the world, are maintained in the balance of rights and responsibilities. All family members 'have duties and responsibilities towards one another and to the family as a whole', which 'vary from member to member because of their natural relationships'.

Bahá'í International Community[6]

Note ye how easily, where unity existeth in a given family, the affairs of that family are conducted; what progress the members of that family make, how they prosper in the world. Their concerns are in order, they enjoy comfort and tranquillity, they are secure, their position is assured, they come to be envied by all. Such a family but addeth to its stature and its lasting honour, as day succeedeth day.

'Abdu'l-Bahá

Dimensions of a Spiritual Marriage

Spirituality

Among the people of Bahá . . . marriage must be a union of the body and of the spirit as well, for here both husband and wife are aglow with the same wine, both are enamoured of the same matchless Face, both live and move through the same spirit, both are illumined by the same glory. This connection between them is a spiritual one, hence it is a bond that will abide forever. Likewise do they enjoy strong and lasting ties in the physical world as well, for if the marriage is based both on the spirit and the body, that union is a true one, hence it will endure. If, however, the bond is physical and nothing more, it is sure to be only temporary, and must inexorably end in separation.

'Abdu'l-Bahá[1]

The best love is the kind that awakens the soul and makes us reach for more, that plants a fire in our hearts and brings peace to our minds.

Nicholas Sparks

The institution of marriage, as established by Bahá'u'lláh, while giving due importance to the physical aspect of marital union, considers it as subordinate to the moral and spiritual purposes and functions with which it has been invested by an All-Wise and loving Providence.

From letter written on behalf of Shoghi Effendi[2]

Spiritual marriage means to marry your soul to the eternal love of God.

Paramhansa Yogananda

Except thou build it, Father,
The house is built in vain,
Except thou, Saviour, bless it,
The joy will turn to pain;
But nought can break the marriage
Of hearts in thee made one,
And love thy Spirit hallows
Is endless love begun.

John Ellerton

Friendship

A good marriage has in it all the pleasures of a friendship, all the enjoyments of sense and reason, and indeed all the sweets of life.

Joseph Addison

Friendship is a deep oneness that develops when two people, speaking the truth in love to one another, journey together to the same horizon.

Timothy Keller[3]

It is not a lack of love, but a lack of friendship that makes unhappy marriages.

Friedrich Nietzsche

It is often said that it is love that makes the world go round. However, without doubt, it is friendship which keeps our spinning existence on an even keel.

True friendship provides so many of the essentials for a happy life – it is the foundation on which to build an enduring relationship, it is the mortar which bonds us together in harmony, and it is the calm, warm protection we sometimes need when the world outside seems cold and chaotic.

True friendship holds a mirror to our foibles and failings, without destroying our sense of worthiness. True friendship nurtures our hopes, supports us in our disappointments, and encourages us to grow to our best potential.

The bride and groom came together as friends. Today, they pledge to each other not only their love, but also the strength, warmth and, most importantly, the fun of true friendship.

Judy Bielicki

In marriage do thou be wise: prefer the person before money, virtue before beauty, the mind before the body; then thou hast a wife, a friend, a companion, a second self.

William Penn

The Lord, peerless is He, hath made woman and man to abide with each other in the closest companionship, and to be even as a single soul. They are two helpmates, two intimate friends, who should be concerned about the welfare of each other.

If they live thus, they will pass through this world with perfect contentment, bliss, and peace of heart, and become the object of divine grace and favour in the Kingdom of heaven . . .

Strive, then, to abide, heart and soul, with each other as two doves in the nest, for this is to be blessed in both worlds.

'Abdu'l-Bahá[4]

Surely, all must today be called to love, to unity and to kindness; to integrity, to friendship, to fellowship and to divine worship. I hope that thou and thy dear husband may continue to serve in all spirit and fragrance and that in this world ye may remain two radiant candles and in the eternal horizon ye may glisten like unto two shining stars.

'Abdu'l-Bahá[5]

Loyalty

Let man and woman, united in marriage, constantly exert themselves, that (they may not be) disunited (and) may not violate their mutual fidelity.

Thus has been declared to you the law for a husband and his wife, which is intimately connected with conjugal happiness, and the manner of raising offspring in times of calamity . . .

Laws of Manu

Faithfulness must mark the relationship of husband and wife.

Hindu scriptures

Chastity implies both before and after marriage an unsullied, chaste sex life. Before marriage absolutely chaste, after marriage absolutely faithful to one's chosen companion. Faithful in all sexual acts, faithful in word and in deed.

From a letter written on behalf of Shoghi Effendi[6]

Equality

When a man has equal partners then I fear not.

Aeschylus

Women and men have been and will always be equal in the sight of God . . . Verily God created women for men, and men for women.

Bahá'u'lláh[7]

The happiness of mankind will be realized when women and men coordinate and advance equally, for each is the complement and helpmeet of the other.

'Abdu'l-Bahá[8]

The man may be the head of the home but the wife is the heart.

Kenyan proverb

. . . men and women alike are the revealers of His names and attributes, and from the spiritual viewpoint there is no difference between them. Whosoever draweth nearer to God, that one is the most favoured, whether man or woman.

'Abdu'l-Bahá[9]

The full measure of intimacy in marriage requires husbands and wives to be equals.

Blaine J. Fowers[10]

Husband and wife are like the two equal parts of a soybean. If the two parts are put under the earth separately, they will not grow. The soybean will grow only when the parts are covered by the skin. Marriage is the skin which covers each of them and makes them one.

Baba Hari Dass

Between husband and wife . . .
all things should be in common
without any distinction
    or means of distinguishing.

Martin Luther

In true marriage lies
Nor equal, nor unequal: each fulfils
Defect in each, and always thought in thought,
Purpose in purpose, will in will, they grow,
The single pure and perfect animal,
The two-ceil'd heart beating,
With one full stroke, Life.

Alfred, Lord Tennyson

Being equitable means being fair about your expectations in a relationship. This may mean sometimes taking turns, going the second mile, or delaying your own gratification to please your partner. Couples who take pleasure in giving as well as receiving have a deeper love and more satisfaction.

Pat Love[11]

Service

A marriage between two souls, alive to the Message of God in this day, dedicated to the service of His Cause, working for the good of humanity, can be a potent force in the lives of others and an example and inspiration to other Bahá'ís, as well as to non-believers.

From a letter written on behalf of Shoghi Effendi[12]

There are literally hundreds of ways to incorporate shared service into your marriage . . . the key is to find something that fits your personal style . . . Our own sense of devotion and intimacy deepens as we secretly observe the results of our service. Two people joined in marriage . . . are ordained to serve others as a team. As a partnership, two people can serve other people better than they could as separate individuals. So don't neglect the practice of shared service. It will do more to enrich the soul of your marriage than you can ever imagine.

Les and Leslie Parrott[13]

. . . every aspect of a person's life is an element of his or her service to Bahá'u'lláh: the love and respect one has for one's parents; the pursuit of one's education; the nurturing of good health; the acquiring of a trade or profession; one's behaviour towards others and the upholding of a high moral standard; one's marriage and the bringing up of one's children; one's activities in teaching the Faith and the building up the strength of the Bahá'í community, whether this be in such simple matters as attending the Nineteen Day Feast or the observance of Bahá'í Holy Days, or in more demanding tasks required by service in the administration of the Faith; and, not least, to take time each day to read the Writings and say the Obligatory Prayer, which are the source of growing spiritual strength, understanding, and attachment to God.

From a message written on behalf of the Universal House of Justice[14]

Service is the magnet which draws the divine confirmations. Thus, when a person is active, they are blessed by the Holy Spirit.

From a letter written on behalf of Shoghi Effendi[15]

He hopes that from now on you and your dear husband will be able to serve the Faith unitedly and devotedly together, as that is the highest form of Bahá'í cooperation in marriage.

From a letter written on behalf of Shoghi Effendi[16]

Respect and Honour One Another

Divine Justice demands that the rights of both sexes should be equally respected since neither is superior to the other in the eyes of Heaven. Dignity before God depends, not on sex, but on purity and luminosity of heart. Human virtues belong equally to all!

'Abdu'l-Bahá[17]

You are my spouse
My feet shall run because of you
My feet shall dance because of you
My heart shall beat because of you
My eyes see because of you
My mind thinks because of you
And I shall love because of you.

Inuit indigenous tribes

Let the wife make the husband glad to come home, and let him make her sorry to see him leave.

Martin Luther

These words do I address to you maidens who are being married, These counsels do I give to you, bridegrooms, Heed them in your minds and lay them to heart. Let each cherish the other with Righteousness. Then surely the reward of a happy life shall be yours.

Zoroaster[18]

Love and respect must reign in every home. This is commended because every member of the household is a soul and as a soul he is worthy of love and respect.

Hindu Scriptures

God in heaven above please protect the ones we love.
We honour all you created,
    as we pledge our hearts and lives together.
We honour mother-earth – and ask for our marriage to
    be abundant and grow stronger through the
        seasons;
We honour fire – and ask that our union
    be warm and glowing with love in our hearts;
We honour wind – and ask we sail through life
    safe and calm as in our father's arms;
We honour water – to clean and soothe our
    relationship –
    that it may never thirst for love;
With all the forces of the universe you created,

we pray for harmony and true happiness as
we forever grow young together.

Cherokee Marriage Prayer

Treat yourselves and each other with respect,
And remind yourselves often of what brought you
    together.
Give the highest priority to the tenderness,
Gentleness and kindness that your connection
    deserves.
When frustration, difficulties and fear assail your
    relationship,
As they threaten all relationships at one time or
    another,
Remember to focus on what is right between you,
Not only the part which seems wrong.
In this way, you can ride out the storms
When clouds hide the face of the sun in your lives. . .
Remembering that even if you lose sight of it for a
    moment,
The sun is still there.
And if each of you takes responsibility for the quality
Of your life together,
It will be marked by abundance and delight.

Apache wedding blessing

One man should love and honour one:
A bride-bed
Theirs alone till life's done.

Euripides

. . . the best way to thank God is to love one another.

'Abdu'l-Bahá[19]

No marriage can survive without the words 'I'm sorry.'
No 'I'm sorry' can survive without a change of behaviour.

Mike Yaconelli

If someone commits an error and wrong toward you, you must instantly forgive him.

'Abdu'l-Bahá[20]

Commitment

Bahá'í marriage is the commitment of the two parties one to the other, and their mutual attachment of mind and heart.

'Abdu'l-Bahá[21]

Love is, above all, the gift of oneself.

Jean Anouilh

Marriage may be compared to a plant that requires daily nurture, daily attention, daily care, and cultivation. It will not develop of its own accord; only as effort and will are exerted will it grow and mature. For a marriage to succeed, both husband and wife must be committed to its success. They must build an enduring love relationship that is centered in the heart of their consciousness. Their relationship must be nurtured with the water of loyalty and love.

Margaret Ruhe[22]

Commitment gives you the opportunity to be truly known by another human being.

Pat Love[23]

Creating a Strong Marriage

Elements of a Strong Marriage

. . . the Cause of the Ancient Beauty is the very essence of love, the very channel of oneness, existing only that all may become the waves of one sea, and bright stars of the same endless sky, and pearls within the shell of singleness, and gleaming jewels quarried from the mines of unity; that they may become servants one to another, adore one another, bless one another, praise one another; that each one may loose his tongue and extol the rest without exception, each one voice his gratitude to all the rest; that all should lift up their eyes to the horizon of glory, and remember that they are linked to the Holy Threshold; that they should see nothing but good in one another, hear nothing but praise of one another, and speak no word of one another save only to praise.

'Abdu'l-Bahá[1]

Marriage has the power to set the course of your life as a whole. If your marriage is strong, even if all the circumstances in your life around you are filled with trouble and weakness, it won't matter. You will be able to move out into the world in strength.

Timothy Keller[2]

The Art of Marriage

A good marriage must be created.

In the marriage, the little things are the big things.

It is never being too old to hold hands.

It is remembering to say 'I love you' at least once
each day,

It is never going to sleep angry.

It is having a mutual sense of values and objectives.

It is standing together and facing the world.

It is forming a circle of love that gathers in the whole
family.

It is speaking words of appreciation and demon-
strating gratitude in thoughtful ways.

It is having the capacity to forgive and forget.

It is giving each other an atmosphere in which each
person can grow.

It is a common search for the good and the beautiful.

It is not only marrying the right person

It is being the right partner.

Wilfred A Peterson

The real act of marriage takes place in the heart, not
in the ballroom or church or synagogue. It's a choice
you make – not just on your wedding day, but over
and over again – and that choice is reflected in the
way you treat your husband or wife.

Barbara De Angelis

A great marriage is not when the 'perfect couple' come together. It is when an imperfect couple learns to enjoy their differences.

Dave Meurer

Marriage is not a noun; it's a verb. It isn't something you get. It's something you do. It's the way you love your partner every day.

Barbara De Angelis

Do not expect too much of marriage, or too little. Water cannot rise above its own level. Your union cannot produce more than you two contribute to it. If you are full of imperfections, intolerant, impatient, exacting, dictatorial, suspicious, short-tempered, selfish, do not imagine that these characteristics are going to make your marriage happy or that by changing your partner a new union will be more successful! Marriage, like all our other relationships in life, is a process which, among other things, serves to grind the sharp edges off us. The grinding often hurts, the adjustment to another person's character is difficult at first, that is why love is needed here more than in any other relationship. Love, being essentially a divine force, binds; it leaps like a spark the gap between people's thoughts and conflicting desires, between perhaps widely different temperaments.

It heals the wounds we all inflict on each other whether inadvertently or in moments of rage, jealousy or spite. To the influence of love in marriage is gradually added another powerful catalyst: habit. The common home, the daily association, produces a common framework, and habit, one of the most powerful forces in life, begins to knit husband and wife together. It acts as a wonderful stabilizer; if love is allowed to fail, habit itself may be strong enough to preserve the union.

Rúḥíyyih Khánum[3]

Communication

A happy marriage is a long conversation . . . that seems all too short.

Andre Maurois

Married couples, who love each other, tell each other a thousand things without talking.

Chinese proverb

The greatest happiness for a lover is to converse with his beloved.

'Abdu'l-Bahá[4]

If I love you, I need not continually speak of my love
– you will know without any words.

'Abdu'l-Bahá[5]

. . . speak with each other with infinite amity and
love.

'Abdu'l-Bahá[6]

Consultation

The heaven of divine wisdom is illumined with the
two luminaries of consultation and compassion.
Take ye counsel together in all matters, inasmuch as
consultation is the lamp of guidance which leadeth
the way, and is the bestower of understanding.

Bahá'u'lláh[7]

The maturity of the gift of understanding is made
manifest through consultation.

Bahá'u'lláh[8]

Strive with all your hearts and with the very power
of life that unity and love may continually increase.
In discussions look toward the reality without being
self-opinionated. Let no one assert and insist upon

his own mere opinion; nay, rather, let each investigate reality with the greatest love and fellowship. Consult upon every matter, and when one presents the point of view of reality itself, that shall be acceptable to all. Then will spiritual unity increase among you, individual illumination will be greater, happiness will be more abundant, and you will draw nearer and nearer to the Kingdom of God.

'Abdu'l-Bahá[9]

Settle all things, both great and small, by consultation. Without prior consultation, take no important step in your own personal affairs. Concern yourselves with one another. Help along one another's projects and plans.

'Abdu'l-Bahá[10]

In all things it is necessary to consult. This matter should be forcibly stressed by thee, so that consultation may be observed by all. The intent of what hath been revealed from the Pen of the Most High is that consultation may be fully carried out among the friends, inasmuch as it is and will always be a cause of awareness and of awakening and a source of good and well-being.

Bahá'u'lláh[11]

The preservation of unity within the family, and the maintenance of a setting in which all members of the family may grow spiritually, requires moderation and restraint by all concerned. Family consultation is a vital element in the development of a sound relationship; the principles of consultation enumerated by the Master, including courtesy, respect for the views of others, and the full and frank expression of opinions, are applicable to relationships within the family . . .

From a letter written on behalf of the Universal House of Justice[12]

. . . consultation is acceptable in the presence of the Almighty, and hath been enjoined upon the believers, so that they may confer upon ordinary and personal matters, as well as on affairs which are general in nature and universal.

'Abdu'l-Bahá[13]

. . . the Faith is intended to strengthen the family, not weaken it, and one of the keys to a strengthening of unity is loving consultation. The atmosphere within a Bahá'í family as within the community as a whole should express 'the keynote of the Cause of God' which, the beloved Guardian has stated, 'is not dictatorial authority, but humble fellowship, not arbitrary power, but the spirit of frank and loving consultation' . . .

In any group, however loving the consultation, there are nevertheless points on which, from time to time, agreement cannot be reached. In a Spiritual Assembly this dilemma is resolved by a majority vote. There can, however, be no majority where only two parties are involved, as in the case of a husband and wife. There are, therefore, times when a wife should defer to her husband, and times when a husband should defer to his wife, but neither should ever unjustly dominate the other. In short, the relationship between husband and wife should be as held forth in the prayer revealed by 'Abdu'l-Bahá which is often read at Bahá'í weddings: 'Verily, they are married in obedience to Thy command. Cause them to become the signs of harmony and unity until the end of time.'

From a letter written on behalf of the Universal House of Justice[14]

You have asked, however, for specific rules of conduct to govern the relationships of husbands and wives. This the House of Justice does not wish to do, and it feels that there is already adequate guidance included in the compilation on this subject; for example, the principle that the rights of each and all in the family unit must be upheld, and the advice that loving consultation should be the keynote, that all matters must be settled in harmony and love, and that there are times when the husband and wife should defer to the wishes of the other. Exactly under what circumstances such deference should take place is a matter for each couple to determine. If, God forbid, they fail to agree, and their disagreement leads to estrangement, they should seek counsel from those they trust and in whose sincerity and sound judgement they have confidence, in order to preserve and strengthen their ties as a united family.

From a letter written on behalf of the Universal House of Justice[15]

Consultation has been ordained by Bahá'u'lláh as the means by which agreement is to be reached and a collective course of action defined. It is applicable to the marriage partners and within the family, and indeed in all areas where believers participate in mutual decision-making. It requires all participants to express their opinions with absolute freedom and without apprehension that they will be censured and/or their views belittled; these prerequisites for success are unattainable if the fear of violence or abuse are present.

From a letter written on behalf of the Universal House of Justice[16]

A Home Together

Blessed is the spot, and the house, and the place, and the city, and the heart, and the mountain, and the refuge, and the cave, and the valley, and the land, and the sea, and the island, and the meadow where mention of God hath been made, and His praise glorified.

Bahá'u'lláh[1]

Blessed is the house that hath attained unto My tender mercy, wherein My remembrance is celebrated, and which is ennobled by the presence of My loved ones, who have proclaimed My praise, cleaved fast to the cord of My grace and been honoured by chanting My verses. Verily they are the exalted servants whom God hath extolled in the Qayyúmu'l-Asmá' and other scriptures. Verily He is the All-Hearing, the Answerer, He Who perceiveth all things.

Bahá'u'lláh[2]

The Lord . . . blesseth the habitation of the just.

Proverbs 3:33

Where we love, is home. Home that our feet may leave, but not our hearts.

Oliver Wendell Holmes

Peace be both to thee, and peace be to thine house, and peace be unto all that thou hast.

1 Samuel 25:6 KJV

. . . if he wish to magnify the Lord, it behoveth him to do so in such places as have been erected for this purpose, or in his own home.

Bahá'u'lláh[3]

My home is the home of peace.
My home is the home of joy and delight.
My home is the home of laughter and exultation.
Whosoever enters through the portals of this home,
    must go out with gladsome heart.
This is the home of light;
    whosoever enters here must become illumined.
This is the home of knowledge;
    the one who enters it must receive knowledge.
This is the home of love:
    those who come in must learn the lessons of love;
    thus may they know how to love each other.

'Abdu'l-Bahá[4]

People who come so close to our doors and perhaps enter our home should not be left to go without carrying away some of the delights we are enjoying.

They are also seeking souls earnestly desiring to attain their spiritual and social ideals.

From a letter written on behalf of Shoghi Effendi[5]

Virtues to be Found in the Home

The home should be a place of mutual understanding and love, of chastity and faithfulness, of reverence for the aged and respect for the young. There should be no selfishness among members of the family.

Buddhist Scriptures

The home should be a place where obedience, peace, love, generosity, humility, truth and righteousness reign. Here children should respect their parents. To such a home will come contentment, knowledge, prosperity and glory.

Zoroastrian Scriptures

If a man in his own home doth not treat his relations and friends with entire trustworthiness and integrity, his dealings with the outside world – no matter how much trustworthiness and honesty he may bring to them – will prove barren and unproductive. First one should order one's own domestic affairs, then attend to one's business with the public . . . Blessed be the soul that shineth with the light of trustworthiness among the people and becometh a sign of perfection amidst all men.

'Abdu'l-Bahá[6]

If you seek immunity from the sway of the forces of the contingent world, hang the 'Most Great Name' in your dwelling, wear the ring of the 'Most Great Name' on your finger, place the picture of 'Abdu'l-Bahá in your home and always recite the prayers that I have written. Then you will behold the marvellous effect they produce.

'Abdu'l-Bahá[7]

Prayers for the Home

I beseech God to graciously make of thy home a centre for the diffusion of the light of divine guidance, for the dissemination of the Words of God and for enkindling at all times the fire of love in the hearts of His faithful servants and maidservants. Know thou of a certainty that every house wherein the anthem of praise is raised to the Realm of Glory in celebration of the Name of God is indeed a heavenly home, and one of the gardens of delight in the Paradise of God.

'Abdu'l-Bahá[8]

O my God! Let the outpourings of Thy bounty and blessings descend upon homes whose inmates have embraced Thy Faith, as a token of Thy grace and as a mark of loving-kindness from Thy presence. Verily unsurpassed art Thou in granting forgiveness. Should Thy bounty be withheld from anyone, how could he be reckoned among the followers of the Faith in Thy Day?

Bless me, O my God, and those who will believe in Thy signs on the appointed Day, and such as cherish my love in their hearts – a love which Thou dost instil into them.

Verily Thou art the Lord of righteousness, the Most Exalted.

The Báb[9]

Verily, I pray God to make thy home a center for the radiation of light and the glowing of His love in the hearts of His people. Know that in every home when God is praised and prayed to, and His Kingdom proclaimed, that home is a garden of God and a paradise of His happiness.

'Abdu'l-Bahá[10]

Fill Thou, O God, our home with harmony and happiness, with laughter and delight, with radiant kindliness and overflowing joy, that in the union of our hearts Thy love may find a lodging place, and Thou Thyself mayst make this home of ours Thine Own!

George Townshend[11]

O God, make Thou this home of ours the garden of affection, a ripening place of love, where the hidden powers of our hearts may unfold, expand and bear the fruit of an abiding joy.

George Townshend[12]

O God, make the door of this house wide enough to receive all who need human love and fellowship; narrow enough to shut out all envy, pride and strife. Make its threshold smooth enough to be no stumbling block to children, nor to straying feet, but rugged and strong enough to turn back the tempter's power. God make the door of this house the gateway to thine eternal kingdom.

Bishop Thomas Ken

Almighty Father, we humbly pray for your blessing upon this home. Accept our offering of thanksgiving for the promise of security and happiness which it represents, and fortify our resolve to make it, now and always, a temple dedicated to you. Let it be filled with the beauty of holiness and the warmth of love. May the guest and stranger find within it welcome and friendship. So may it ever merit the praise: 'How lovely are your tents, O Jacob, your dwelling places, O Israel.'

Service of the Heart

Let my food, O my Lord, be Thy beauty, and my drink the light of Thy presence, and my hope Thy pleasure, and my work Thy praise, and my companion Thy remembrance, and my aid Thy sovereignty, and my dwelling-place Thy habitation, and my home the seat which Thou hast exalted above the limitations of them that are shut out as by a veil from Thee.

Thou art, in truth, the God of power, of strength and glory.

Bahá'u'lláh[13]

Returning Safely to Home

Home is the place where, when you have to go there,
     They have to take you in.

Robert Frost[14]

O God, my God! I have set out from my home, holding fast unto the cord of Thy love, and I have committed myself wholly to Thy care and Thy protection. I entreat Thee by Thy power through which Thou didst protect Thy loved ones from the wayward and the perverse, and from every contumacious oppressor, and every wicked doer who hath strayed far from Thee, to keep me safe by Thy bounty and Thy grace. Enable me, then, to return to my home by Thy power and Thy might. Thou art, truly, the Almighty, the Help in Peril, the Self-Subsisting.

Bahá'u'lláh[15]

I have risen this morning by Thy grace, O my God, and left my home trusting wholly in Thee, and committing myself to Thy care. Send down, then, upon me, out of the heaven of Thy mercy, a blessing from Thy side, and enable me to return home in safety even as Thou didst enable me to set out under Thy protection with my thoughts fixed steadfastly upon Thee.

There is none other God but Thee, the One, the Incomparable, the All-Knowing, the All-Wise.

Bahá'u'lláh[16]

O Lord! Whether travelling or at home, and in my occupation or in my work, I place my whole trust in Thee.

The Báb[17]

Hospitality

Make your house a haven of rest and peace. Be hospitable, and let the doors of your house be open to the faces of friends and strangers. Welcome every guest with radiant grace and let each feel that it is his own home . . .

O beloved of God, may your home be a vision of the paradise of Abhá, so that whosoever enters there may feel the essence of purity and harmony, and cry out from the heart: 'Here is the home of love! Here is the palace of love! Here is the nest of love! Here is the garden of love!'

Attributed to 'Abdu'l-Bahá[18]

. . . thank ye God that ye have made your home a Bahá'í centre and a gathering place for the friends.

'Abdu'l-Bahá[19]

Blessed art thou for having opened the door of thy home unto the people to come and hear of the Kingdom.

'Abdu'l-Bahá[20]

The Spiritual Home

This is a spiritual house, the home of the spirit. There is no discord here; all is love and unity. When souls are gathered together in this way, the divine bestowals descend.

'Abdu'l-Bahá[21]

Suffer thy home to become a nest for the dove of the Holy Spirit and thine eye the mirror for the reflection of the Beauty of the Almighty.

'Abdu'l-Bahá[22]

The upbuilding of a home, the bringing of joy and comfort into human hearts are truly glories of mankind.

'Abdu'l-Bahá[23]

Creating a Bahá'í Home

In this glorious Cause the life of a married couple should resemble the life of the angels in heaven – a life full of joy and spiritual delight, a life of unity and concord, a friendship both mental and physical. The home should be orderly and well-organized. Their ideas and thoughts should be like the rays of the sun of truth and the radiance of the brilliant stars in the heavens. Even as two birds they should warble melodies upon the branches of the tree of fellowship and harmony. They should always be elated with joy and gladness and be a source of happiness to the hearts of others. They should set an example to their fellow-men, manifest true and sincere love towards each other and educate their children in such a manner as to blazon the fame and glory of their family.

'Abdu'l-Bahá[24]

A truly Bahá'í home is a true fortress upon which the Cause can rely while planning its campaigns. If [a man and a woman] love each other and would like to marry, Shoghi Effendi does not wish them to think that by doing so they are depriving themselves of the privilege of service; in fact such a union will enhance their ability to serve. There is nothing more beautiful than to have young Bahá'ís marry and found truly Bahá'í homes, the type Bahá'u'lláh wishes them to be . . .

From a letter written on behalf of Shoghi Effendi[25]

The task of bringing up a Bahá'í child, as emphasized time and again in Bahá'í writings, is the chief responsibility of the mother, whose unique privilege is indeed to create in her home such conditions as would be most conducive to both his material and spiritual welfare and advancement.

From a letter written on behalf of Shoghi Effendi[26]

. . . the home is an institution that Bahá'u'lláh has come to strengthen and not to weaken . . . Serve the Cause but also remember your duties towards your home. It is for you to find the balance and see that neither makes you neglect the other.

From a letter written on behalf of Shoghi Effendi[27]

A Home of Unity

. . . pray to Bahá'u'lláh to help unite you with your husband and make your home a true and happy home.

From a letter written on behalf of Shoghi Effendi[28]

It is one of the essential teachings of the Faith that unity should be maintained in the home. Of course this does not mean that any member of the family has a right to influence the faith of any other member; and if this is realized by all the members, then it seems certain that unity would be feasible.

From a letter written on behalf of Shoghi Effendi[29]

When the friends begin to have peace at home they can teach the people to have peace between the nations and classes.

From a letter written on behalf of Shoghi Effendi[30]

Becoming a Family

When Children Come

As to thy question concerning the husband and wife, the tie between them and the children given to them by God: Know thou, verily, the husband is one who hath sincerely turned unto God, is awakened by the call of the Beauty of El-Baha and chanteth the verses of Oneness in the great assemblies; the wife is a being who wisheth to be overflowing with and seeketh after the attributes of God and His names; and the tie between them is none other than the Word of God. Verily, it causeth the multitudes to assemble together and the remote ones to be united. Thus the husband and wife are brought into affinity, are united and harmonized, even as though they were one person. Through their mutual union, companionship and love great results are produced in the world, both material and spiritual. The spiritual result is the appearance of divine bounties. The material result is the children who are born in the cradle of the love of God, who are nurtured by the breast of the knowledge of God, and who are brought up in the bosom of the gift of God, and who are fostered in the lap of the training of God. Such children are those of whom it was said by Christ, 'Verily, they are the children of the Kingdom!'

'Abdu'l-Bahá[1]

Every child comes with the message that God is not yet discouraged of man.

Rabindranath Tagore

. . . have for [your chidren] an abundant love and exert thine utmost in training them, so that their being may grow through the milk of the love of God, forasmuch as it is the duty of parents to perfectly and thoroughly train their children.

'Abdu'l-Bahá[2]

Give this child a good education; make every effort that it may have the best you can afford, so that it may be enabled to enjoy the advantage of this glorious age. Do all you can to encourage spirituality in them.

'Abdu'l-Bahá[3]

O maid-servants of the Merciful! It is incumbent upon you to train the children from their earliest babyhood! It is incumbent upon you to beautify their morals! It is incumbent upon you to attend to them under all aspects and circumstances, inasmuch as God – glorified and exalted is He! – hath ordained mothers to be the primary trainers of children and infants. This is a great and important affair and a

high and exalted position, and it is not allowable to
slacken therein at all!

If thou walkest in this right path, thou wouldst
become a real mother to the children, both spiritu-
ally and materially. I beg God to make thee severed
from this world, attracted to the fragrances of sanc-
tity which are being diffused from the garden of the
Kingdom of El-ABHA, and a servant of the Cause of
God in the vineyard of God.

'Abdu'l-Bahá[4]

Teach ye your children so that they may peruse the
divine verses every morn and eve. God hath pre-
scribed unto every father to educate his children,
both boys and girls, in the sciences and in morals,
and in crafts and professions . . .

Bahá'u'lláh[5]

You are the children of whom Christ has said, 'Of
such is the kingdom of God'; and according to the
words of Bahá'u'lláh you are the very lamps or candles
of the world of humanity, for your hearts are exceed-
ingly pure and your spirits most sensitive. You are near
the source; you have not yet become contaminated.
You are the lambs of the heavenly Shepherd. You are
as polished mirrors reflecting pure light. My hope is
that your parents may educate you spiritually and

give you thorough moral training. May you develop so that each one of you shall become imbued with all the virtues of the human world. May you advance in all material and spiritual degrees. May you become learned in sciences, acquire the arts and crafts, prove to be useful members of human society and assist the progress of human civilization. May you be a cause of the manifestation of divine bestowals – each one of you a shining star radiating the light of the oneness of humanity toward the horizons of the East and West. May you be devoted to the love and unity of mankind, and through your efforts may the reality deposited in the human heart find its divine expression. I pray for you, asking the assistance and confirmation of God in your behalf.

You are all my children, my spiritual children. Spiritual children are dearer than physical children, for it is possible for physical children to turn away from the Spirit of God, but you are spiritual children and, therefore, you are most beloved. I wish for you progress in every degree of development. May God assist you. May you be surrounded by the beneficent light of His countenance, and may you attain maturity under His nurture and protection. You are all blessed.

'Abdu'l-Bahá[6]

The greatest benefit which we have to confer on you is: Guidance to God.

When God chose us to be your parents He commanded us to offer you this guidance. Therefore, it is by His will that we give you His Holy Teaching. We speak to you of Him and of His prophets, we surround you continually with thoughts of faith and worship, and we never cease to pray for you. We cannot compel you to learn the lessons which we teach; we would not compel you if we could, for God intends our wills to be free. You must choose for yourself. Your mother and I are trying – as best we may – to follow the leading of that Guidance, and it is our hope and prayer that you will travel with us. We should be very lonely if we had to take one step without you. For this teaching which God has given us to pass on to you is the most precious thing we have to give you: more precious far than food, or clothes or schooling, or even life itself – for this knowledge is ETERNAL life.

George Townshend[7]

To every child – I dream of a world where you can laugh, dance, sing, learn, live in peace and be happy.

Malala Yousafzai

Being a Family

The family is a unit and should beseech God as one.

Qur'án

If love and agreement are manifest in a single family, that family will advance, become illumined and spiritual.

'Abdu'l-Bahá[8]

If the members of a family are perfectly united it will add to their comfort and joy.

'Abdu'l-Bahá[9]

A happy family is but an earlier heaven.
George Bernard Shaw

According to the teachings of Bahá'u'lláh the family, being a human unit, must be educated according to the rules of sanctity. All the virtues must be taught the family. The integrity of the family bond must be constantly considered, and the rights of the individual members must not be transgressed. The rights of the son, the father, the mother – none of them must be transgressed, none of them must be arbitrary. Just as the son has certain obligations to his father, the father, likewise, has certain obligations to his son. The mother, the sister and other members of the household have their certain prerogatives. All these rights and prerogatives must be conserved, yet the unity of the family must be sustained. The injury of one shall be considered the injury of all; the comfort of each, the comfort of all; the honour of one, the honour of all.

'Abdu'l-Bahá[10]

If you can say that you have built genuinely loving relationships with a spouse and children, then you have already succeeded in accomplishing more than most people accomplish in a lifetime.

M. Scott Peck[11]

The family is one of nature's masterpieces.

George Santayana

The relationship between family members represents a complex of mutual and complementary duties and responsibilities that are implemented within the framework of the Bahá'í ideal of family life and are conducive to its unity. The concept of a Bahá'í family is based on the principle that the man is charged with the responsibility of supporting the entire family financially, and the woman is the chief and primary educator of the children. This does not mean that these functions are inflexibly fixed and cannot be changed and adjusted to suit particular family situations. Furthermore, while primary responsibility is assigned, it is anticipated that fathers would play a significant role in the education of the children and women would be breadwinners.

From a letter written on behalf of the Universal House of Justice[12]

Note ye how easily, where unity existeth in a given family, the affairs of that family are conducted; what progress the members of that family make, how they prosper in the world. Their concerns are in order, they enjoy comfort and tranquillity, they are secure, their position is assured, they come to be envied by all. Such a family but addeth to its stature and its lasting honour, as day succeedeth day

'Abdu'l-Bahá[13]

Families are the compass that guides us. They are the inspiration to reach great heights, and our comfort when we occasionally falter.

Brad Henry

In family life, love is the oil that eases friction, the cement that binds closer together, and the music that brings harmony.

Friedrich Nietzsche

If thou become firm and steadfast in the love of God, thou shalt be confirmed with a confirmation whereby thy face will be gladdened, thy heart rejoiced and all thy family will be happy and pleased.

'Abdu'l-Bahá[14]

I beg of God that thou mayest be so assisted in serving the Holy Threshold that all thy family will be astonished and amazed, and will glory and honour.

'Abdu'l-Bahá[15]

I ask from the favours of the Sun of Truth the splendours of the eternal outpouring for thee; I beg everlasting glory and desire for thee and thy family divine gifts, so that all of you may become united and harmonized, rest under the shade of the Tree of Life, and become eternal and established in the Kingdom of Being.

'Abdu'l-Bahá[16]

Rejoice with your family in the beautiful land of life.

Albert Einstein

A Marriage of Joy, Play and Laughter

Joy and Happiness

Hail wedded love, mysterious law, true source of human happiness.

John Milton

There is no more lovely, friendly and charming relationship, communion or company than a good marriage.

Martin Luther

The fulfilment of marriage is that joy in which each lover's true being is flowering because its growth is being welcomed and unconsciously encouraged by the other in the infinite series of daily decisions which is their life together.

J. Neville Ward

Happiness requires something to do,
something to love and something to hope for.

Swahili proverb

Ye are the angels, if your feet be firm, your spirits rejoiced, your secret thoughts pure, your eyes consoled, your ears opened, your breasts dilated with joy, and your souls gladdened, and if you arise to assist the Covenant . . .

'Abdu'l-Bahá[1]

May you be given life! May the rain of the Divine Mercy and the warmth of the Sun of Truth make your gardens fruitful, so that many beautiful flowers of exquisite fragrance and love may blossom in abundance. Turn your faces away from the contemplation of your own finite selves and fix your eyes upon the Everlasting Radiance; then will your souls receive in full measure the Divine Power of the Spirit and the Blessings of the Infinite Bounty.

If you thus keep yourselves in readiness, you will become to the world of humanity a burning flame, a star of guidance, and a fruitful tree, changing all its darkness and woe into light and joy by the shining of the Sun of Mercy and the infinite blessings of the Glad Tidings.

This is the meaning of the power of the Holy Spirit, which I pray may be bountifully showered upon you.

'Abdu'l-Bahá[2]

Marriage is like watching the colour of leaves in the fall; ever changing and more stunningly beautiful with each passing day.

Fawn Weaver

Our wedding was many years ago . . .
The celebration continues to this day.
Gene Perret

The world needs more happiness and illumination. The star of happiness is in every heart, we must remove the clouds so that it may twinkle radiantly. Happiness is an eternal condition. When it is once established, man will ascend to the supreme heights of bliss. A truly happy man will not be subject to the shifting eventualities of time. Like unto an eternal king he will sit upon the throne of fixed realities. He will be impervious to outward, changing circumstances, and through his deeds and actions impart happiness to others. A Bahá'í must be happy, for the blessings of God are bestowed upon him.

Every soul must strive to impart to mankind that joy and happiness the nature of which is permanent.
Attributed to 'Abdu'l-Bahá[3]

The beloved of God must each be the essence of purity and holiness; so may they be known by their purity, freedom and meekness in every land; they may drink from the eternal chalice of the love of God, enjoy its ecstasy, and through meeting the Beauty of Abhá, they should be joyful, active, aglow with zeal and wonderful. This is the station of the sincere. This is the quality of those who are firm. This is the illumination of the faces of those who are near.

'Abdu'l-Bahá[4]

I ask and supplicate God to make you two convinced souls, to bring you forth with such a steadfastness that each of you may withstand the people of a country, and to intoxicate you with the wine of the love of God so that you may cause your hearers to dance, to be joyful and to exult.

This is the time of happiness; it is the day of cheerfulness and exhilaration. For, praise to God, all the doors are opened through the bounty of the Glorious Beauty. But one must show forth perseverance and self-devotion and consecrate his thoughts, until the tree of hope may give fruit and produce consequences.

'Abdu'l-Bahá[5]

My soul doth sense the fragrant breath
Of a well-beloved soul:
The fragrance of that kindly friend
Who's my heart's desire and goal.
The duty of long years of love obey,
And tell the tale of blissful days gone by,
That land and sky may laugh aloud today,
And it may gladden mind and heart and eye.

Rumi[6]

Enkindle with all your might in every meeting the light of the love of God, gladden and cheer every heart with the utmost loving-kindness, show forth your love to the strangers just as you show forth to your relations.

'Abdu'l-Bahá[7]

A Joyful Social Life

Whensoever ye be invited to a banquet or festive occasion, respond with joy and gladness, and whoever fulfilleth his promise will be safe from reproof. This is a Day on which each of God's wise decrees hath been expounded.

Bahá'u'lláh[8]

A healthy social life and Bahá'í work can go hand in hand . . .

Shoghi Effendi[9]

Wherever a Bahá'í community exists, whether large or small, let it be distinguished for its abiding sense of security and faith, its high standard of rectitude, its complete freedom from all forms of prejudice, the spirit of love among its members and for the closely knit fabric of its social life.

The Universal House of Justice[10]

Rest and Relaxation

. . . you should not neglect your health, but con-
sider it the means which enables you to serve. It – the
body – is like a horse which carries the personality
and spirit, and as such should be well cared for so it
can do its work! You should certainly safeguard your
nerves, and force yourself to take time, and not only
for prayer meditation, but for real rest and relaxation.
   From a letter written on behalf of Shoghi Effendi[11]

The most relaxing recreating forces are a healthy reli-
gion, sleep, music, and laughter. Have faith in God
– learn to sleep well – love good music – see the
funny side of life – and health and happiness will be
yours.

Dale Carnegie[12]

Amusement is for the sake of relaxation, and relaxa-
tion is of necessity sweet, for it is the remedy of pain
caused by toil; and intellectual enjoyment is univer-
sally acknowledged to contain an element not only
of the noble but of the pleasant, for happiness is
made up of both.

Aristotle[13]

Playfulness

For some people, 'Playfulness . . . sounds frivolous and shallow, distracting and irrelevant, inefficient and unproductive. That's because we live in a technological culture that worships busyness and activity. Under the guise of saving time, we now are inundated with e-mail . . . and cellular phones. We end each day smothered by the demands of our time and are greeted each new morn with more to do, not less.

Play? There's no time to play. How can we play when the mountain of work and problems we are faced with each day get higher and deeper? How can we play when the world is overcome with poverty, famine, and war?

Play is an expression of God's presence in the world; one clear sign of God's absence in society is the absence of playfulness and laughter. Play is not an escape; it is the way to release the life-smothering grip of busyness, stress, and anxiety. Playfulness is a modern expression of hope.

Michael Yaconelli[14]

. . . being an adult is great for getting things done and handling life's mature responsibilities, but grownups typically forget how to play well. When two married adults can make room in their relationship to play wholeheartedly with childlike abandon – while keeping an adult mindset safely nearby to assure that all necessary responsibilities get handled – their marriage remains fresh and their spirits stay young.

Robert S. Paul[15]

The key to effective play . . . has less to do with *what* we do and more to do with the *spirit* in which we do it. If we approach a moment with a lighthearted attitude, many endeavours can become playful. In fact, playfulness can be an addition to activities and situations normally seen as everyday routine, like washing the car. The benefit: Playfulness adds a spark of energy to almost anything we do.

Play adds the element of enjoyment to our activities by pulling us toward being present in the moment. It may include a degree of spontaneity, creativity, humour, excitement, challenge, or silliness. A playful heart brings a measure of lightness, even in moments filled with seriousness.

Robert S. Paul[16]

Laughter

Give us a sense of humour, Lord, and also things to laugh about. Give us the grace to take a joke against ourselves, and to see the funny side of the things we do. Save us from annoyance, bad temper, resentfulness against our friends. Help us to laugh even in the face of trouble. Fill our minds with love . . .

A.G. Bullivant

I remember a luncheon party in Dublin, to which came a number of these Summer residents to meet 'Abdu'l-Bahá . . .

[The hostess] wanted her party to be a success, of course, but the more she wished these friends to get a glimpse, if only a glimpse, of that World of Reality into which 'Abdu'l-Bahá had ushered her . . .

Most of those present at this luncheon party knew a little of 'Abdu'l-Bahá's life history, and, presumably, were expecting a dissertation from Him on the Bahá'í Cause.

The hostess had suggested to the Master that He speak to them on the subject of Immortality. However, as the meal progressed, and no more than the usual commonplaces of polite society were mentioned, the hostess made an opening, as she thought, for 'Abdu'l-Bahá to speak on spiritual things.

His response to this was to ask if He might tell them a story, and he related one of the Oriental tales, of which He had a great store, and at its conclusion all laughed heartily.

The ice was broken. Others added stories of which the Master's anecdote had reminded them.

Then 'Abdu'l-Bahá, His face beaming with happiness, told another story, and another. His laughter rang through the room.

He said that the Orientals, had many such stories illustrating different phases of life. Many of them are extremely humorous. It is good to laugh. Laughter is a spiritual relaxation. When they were in prison, He said, and under the utmost deprivation and difficulties, each of them at the close of the day would relate the most ludicrous event which had happened. Sometimes it was a little difficult to find one but always they would laugh until the tears would roll down their cheeks. Happiness, He said, is never dependent upon material surroundings, otherwise how sad those years would have been. As it was they were always in the utmost state of joy and happiness.

That was the nearest approach He came to any reference to Himself or to the Divine Teachings. But over that group before the gathering dispersed, hovered a hush and reverence which no learned dissertation would have caused in them.

Howard Colby Ives[17]

I want you to be happy . . . to laugh, smile and rejoice in order that others may be made happy by you.

'Abdu'l-Bahá[18]

Laughter is caused by the slackening or relaxation of the nerves. It is an ideal condition and not physical. Laughter is the visible effect of an invisible cause. For example, happiness and misery are super-sensuous phenomena. One cannot hear them with his ears or touch them with his hands. Happiness is a spiritual state. But happiness is caused either by looking at a beautiful picture, or witnessing a delectable panorama, or associating with the person whom you love, or listening to a good voice, or solving an intellectual problem. All these are the motives of happiness, but the real cause is spiritual.

'Abdu'l-Bahá[19]

Even as the clouds let us shed down tears, and as the lightning flashes let us laugh at our coursings through east and west. By day, by night, let us think but of spreading the sweet savours of God. Let us not keep on forever with our fancies and illusions, with our analysing and interpreting and circulating of complex dubieties. Let us put aside all thoughts of self; let us close our eyes to all on earth, let us neither make known our sufferings nor complain of our wrongs. Rather let us become oblivious of our own selves, and drinking down the wine of heavenly grace, let us cry out our joy, and lose ourselves in the beauty of the All-Glorious.

'Abdu'l-Bahá[20]

Humour too, as you say, is an essential element in preserving a proper balance in this life and in our comprehension of reality.

From a letter written on behalf of the Universal House of Justice[21]

The duty of long years of love obey
And tell the tale of happy days gone by,
That land and sky may laugh aloud today,
And it may gladden mind and heart and eye.

Rumi[22]

Humour, happiness, joy are characteristics of a true Bahá'í life. Frivolity palls and eventually leads to boredom and emptiness, but true happiness and joy and humour that are parts of a balanced life that includes serious thought, compassion and humble servitude to God are characteristics that enrich life and add to its radiance.

From a letter written on behalf of the Universal House of Justice[23]

In Times of Difficulty

If thy daily living become difficult, soon thy Lord will bestow upon thee that which shall satisfy thee. Be patient in the time of affliction and trial, endure every difficulty and hardship with a dilated heart, attracted spirit and eloquent tongue in remembrance of the Merciful. Verily this is the life of satisfaction, the spiritual existence, heavenly repose, divine benediction and the celestial table! Soon the Lord will extenuate thy straightened circumstances even in this world.

'Abdu'l-Bahá[1]

. . . turn your thoughts away from the things which upset you, and constantly pray to Bahá'u'lláh to help you. Then you will find how that pure love, enkindled by God, which burns in the soul when we read and study the Teachings, will warm and heal, more than anything else. Each of us is responsible for one life only, and that is our own. Each of us is immeasurably far from being 'perfect as our heavenly father is perfect' and the task of perfecting our own life and character is one that requires all our attention, our will-power and energy . . .

From a letter written on behalf of the Universal House of Justice[2]

A marriage is like a long trip in a tiny row boat: if one passenger starts to rock the boat, the other has to steady it, otherwise, they will go to the bottom together.

David Reuben

We often feel that our happiness lies in a certain direction; and yet, if we have to pay too heavy a price for it in the end we may discover that we have not really purchased either freedom or happiness, but just some new situation of frustration and disillusion.

From a letter written on behalf of Shoghi Effendi[3]

O beloved of God! Is there any giver save God? He chooseth for His mercy whomsoever He desireth.

He shall open unto you the doors of His knowledge, fill your hearts with His love, rejoice your spirits by the wafting of His holy fragrances, illumine your faces by the Manifest Light and elevate your names among the people.

'Abdu'l-Bahá[4]

Verily, I read thy beautiful composed letter and thank God for that He granted thee characteristics, attributes and deeds which made thee dear and loved by the maid-servants of God . . . Thank God for that He confirmed thee by this wonderful bounty, and, verily, I supplicate unto Him to strengthen thee in rendering this great service in His great vineyard, and to strengthen thy respected husband in patience and forbearance in this test which will pass away, by the help of God, and the veil be removed; difficulty will be replaced by ease; hardship and trouble be changed into comfort, in the shadow of His great Kingdom.

'Abdu'l-Bahá[5]

When such difference of opinion and belief occurs between husband and wife it is very unfortunate for undoubtedly it detracts from that spiritual bond which is the stronghold of the family bond, especially in times of difficulty. The way, however, that it could be remedied is not by acting in such wise as to alienate the other party. One of the objects of the Cause is actually to bring about a closer bond in the homes. In all such cases, therefore, the Master used to advise obedience to the wishes of the other party and prayer. Pray that your husband may gradually see the light and at the same time so act as to draw him nearer rather than prejudice him. Once that harmony is secured then you will be able to serve unhampered.

From a letter written on behalf of Shoghi Effendi to an individual[6]

A good marriage is the union of two good forgivers.

Ruth Bell Graham

Noting that you and your husband have consulted about your family problems with your Spiritual Assembly but did not receive any advice, and also discussed your situation with a family counsellor without success, the House of Justice feels it most essential for your husband and you to understand that marriage can be a source of well-being, conveying a sense of security and spiritual happiness. However, it is not something that just happens. For marriage to become a haven of contentment it requires the cooperation of the marriage partners themselves, and the assistance of their families. You mention your concern over your eldest daughter. It is suggested that you include her and perhaps your younger children in family consultations. As Bahá'ís we understand the importance of the consultative process and we should not feel it is to be used only by the Spiritual Assemblies.

From a letter written on behalf of the Universal House of Justice[7]

The Guardian . . . has learned with deep concern of your family difficulties and troubles. He wishes me to assure you of his fervent prayers on your behalf and on behalf of your dear ones at home, that you may be guided and assisted from on High to compose your differences and to restore complete harmony and fellowship in your midst. While he would urge you to make any sacrifice in order to bring about unity in your family, he wishes you not to feel discouraged if your endeavours do not yield any immediate fruit. You should do your part with absolute faith that in doing so you are fulfilling your duty as a Bahá'í. The rest is assuredly in God's hand.

As regards your husband's attitude towards the Cause: unfriendly though that may be, you should always hope that, through conciliatory and friendly means, and with wise, tactful and patient effort you can gradually succeed in winning his sympathy for the Faith. Under no circumstances should you try to dictate and impose upon him by force your personal religious convictions. Neither should you allow his opposition to the Cause [to] seriously hinder your activities . . . You should act patiently, tactfully and with confidence that your efforts are being guided and reinforced by Bahá'u'lláh.

From a letter written on behalf of Shoghi Effendi[8]

Marriage Through Life's Stages

Young Marriage

There is nothing more beautiful than to have young Bahá'ís marry and found truly Bahá'í homes . . .
From a letter written on behalf of Shoghi Effendi[1]

The Bahá'í youth . . . should be advised, nay even encouraged, to contract marriage while still young and in full possession of their physical vigour. Economic factors, no doubt, are often a serious hindrance to early marriage but in most cases are only an excuse, and as such should not be over stressed.
From a letter written on behalf of Shoghi Effendi[2]

May joy be increased to you as the years go by, and may you become thriving trees bearing delicious and fragrant fruits which are the blessings in the path of service.
Words attributed to 'Abdu'l-Bahá at the marriage of two young Bahá'ís in London in 1911[3]

It is highly important for man to raise a family. So long as he is young, because of youthful self-complacency, he does not realize its significance, but this will be a source of regret when he grows old . . .
'Abdu'l-Bahá[4]

Beginnings are easy, but after that, happiness takes some work.

Liz Thebart, 'Walk Away'

The Passing Years

True love is eternal, infinite, and always like itself. It is equal and pure, without violent demonstrations: it is seen with white hairs and is always young in the heart.

Honoré de Balzac

This bond of common service to the Cause . . . he hopes, and indeed will fervently pray, will be further cemented by the passing of years and through your increased and joint participation in the teaching work . . .

From a letter written on behalf of Shoghi Effendi[5]

Marriage is not a static state between two unchanging people. Marriage is a psychological and spiritual journey that begins in the ecstasy of attraction, meanders through a rocky stretch of self-discovery, and culminates in the creation of an intimate, joyful, lifelong union.

Harville Hendrix

Three Loves in a Life

. . . In youth I saw but a maiden fair;
And finding beauty I sought no more,
But loved and wedded as youth will dare,
And knew little of the prize I bore.
Proud was I 'midst my fellow-men
Dear to me was my young wife then.

But as life advanced and cares came thick –
On every side came pressing round
Till my wearied heart grew faint and sick –
Ever her at my side I found,
With words of counsel wise and free;
Dearer still was she then to me.

Her hair is grey, and her sweet blue eyes,
Though loving still, are no longer bright;
And I list not now for her thoughts so wise;
But far stronger ties our hearts unite.
Dear through life has she ever been;
Dearest now at its close serene.

Anonymous

Mature Marriage

The question is asked:
    'Is there anything more beautiful in life than a
young couple clasping hands and pure hearts in the

path of marriage? Can there be anything more beautiful than young love?'

And the answer is given:

'Yes, there is a more beautiful thing. It is the spectacle of an old man and an old woman finishing their journey together on that path. Their hands are gnarled but still clasped; their faces are seamed but still radiant; their hearts are physically bowed and tired but still strong with love and devotion.

'Yes, there is a more beautiful thing than young love. Old love.'

Anonymous

Same old slippers
Same old rice
Same old glimpse of paradise
                    William James Lampton

The Worn Wedding-Ring

Your wedding-ring wears thin, dear wife; ah, summers
    not a few
Since I put it on your finger first, have pass' o'er me
    and you;
And, love, what changes we have seen – what cares
    and pleasures too,
Since you became my own dear wife, when this old
    ring was new.

O blessings on that happy day, the happiest of my
    life,
When, thanks to God, your low sweet, 'yes' made
    you my loving wife;
Your heart will say the same, I know; that day's as
    dear to you,
That day that made me yours, dear wife, when this
    old ring was new.

How well do I remember now your sweet face that
    day:
How fair you were – how dear you were – my tongue
    could hardly say,
Now how I doted on you; ah, how proud I was of
    you,
But did I love you more than now, when this old ring
    was new?

No – no; no fairer were you then than at this hour
    to me,
And, dear as life to me this day, how could you
    dearer be?
As sweet your face might be that day as now it is, 'tis
    true,
But did I know your heart as well when this old ring
    was new?
O partner of my gladness, wife; what care, what grief
    is there,

For me you would not bravely face, with me you
    would not share?
O what a weary want had every day, if wanting you,
Wanting the love that God made mine when this old
    ring was new.

Years bring fresh links to bind us, wife – young voices
    that are here,
Young faces round our fire that make their mother's
    yet more dear,
Young, loving hearts, your care each day makes yet
    more like to you,
More like the loving heart made mine when this old
    ring was new.

And, bless'd be God! all He has given are with us yet;
    around
Our table, every precious life lent to us, still is found;
Though cares we've known, with hopeful hearts the
    worst we've struggled through;
Bless'd be His name for all His love since this old
    ring was new!

The past is dear; its sweetness still our memories
    treasure yet;
The griefs we're borne, together borne, we would not
    now forget;
Whatever, wife, the future bring, heart unto heart
    still true,

We'll share as we have shared all else since this old
    ring was new.

And if God spare us 'mongst our sons and daughters
    to grow old,
We know His goodness will not let your heart or
    mine grow cold;
Your agèd eyes will see in mine all they've still shown
    to you,
And mine in yours all they have seen since this old
    ring was new.

And O, when death shall come at last to bid me to
    my rest,
May I die looking in those eyes, and resting on that
    breast;
O may my parting gaze be bless'd with the dear sight
    of you,
Of those fond eyes – fond as they were when this old
    ring was new.

W.C. Bennett

I have lived long enough to know that the evening
glow of love has its own riches and splendour.

Benjamin Disraeli

One of the good things that come of a true marriage is, that there is one face on which changes come without you seeing them; or rather, there is one face which you can see the same, through all the shadows which years have gathered upon it.

George Macdonald

A Marriage Ring
The ring, so worn as you behold.
So thin, so pale, is yet of gold:
The passion such it was to prove –
Worn with life's care, love yet was love.

George Crabbe

Love is like a little old woman and a little old man who are still friends even after they know each other so well.

Tommy, age 6

Together Forever

I think a man and woman should choose each other for life, for the simple reason that a long life with all its accidents is barely enough time for a man and woman to understand each other. And to understand is to love.

Mark Twain

If thou desirest eternal life, inhale the heavenly fragrance; and if thou seekest life everlasting, abide beneath the shelter of the Word of God.

'Abdu'l-Bahá[1]

. . . husband and wife should be united both physically and spiritually, that they may ever improve the spiritual life of each other, and may enjoy everlasting unity throughout all the worlds of God.

'Abdu'l-Bahá[2]

Say not 'Good-night' but in some brighter clime, bid me 'Good-morning'.

Anna Laetitia Barbauld

Unable are the loved to die. For love is immortality.

Emily Dickinson

I Heard Your Voice in the Wind Today

I heard your voice in the wind today
and I turned to see your face;
The warmth of the wind caressed me
as I stood silently in place.

I felt your touch in the sun today
as its warmth filled the sky;
I closed my eyes for your embrace
and my spirit soared high.

I saw your eyes in the window pane
as I watched the falling rain;
It seemed as each raindrop fell
it quietly said your name.

I held you close in my heart today
it made me feel complete;
You may have died . . . but you are not gone
you will always be a part of me.

As long as the sun shines . . .
the wind blows . . .
the rain falls . . .
You will live on inside of me forever
for that is all my heart knows.

Anonymous

Those who have passed on through death, have a sphere of their own. It is not removed from ours; their work, the work of the Kingdom, is ours; but it is sanctified from what we call 'time and place'. Time with us is measured by the sun. When there is no more sunrise, and no more sunset, that kind of time does not exist for man. Those who have ascended have different attributes from those who are still on earth, yet there is no real separation.

In prayer there is a mingling of station, a mingling of condition. Pray for them as they pray for you!

'Abdu'l-Bahá[3]

Replying to another questioner, he said that when two people, husband and wife for instance, have been completely united in this life their souls being as one soul, then after one of them has passed away, this union of heart and soul would remain unbroken.

'Abdu'l-Bahá[4]

Do not stand at my grave and cry
I am not there.
I did not die.

Anonymous

Death is Nothing at All

Death is nothing at all.
I have only slipped away to the next room.
I am I and you are you.
Whatever we were to each other,
That, we still are.

Call me by my old familiar name.
Speak to me in the easy way
which you always used.
Put no difference into your tone.
Wear no forced air of solemnity or sorrow.

Laugh as we always laughed
at the little jokes we enjoyed together.
Play, smile, think of me. Pray for me.
Let my name be ever the household word
that it always was.
Let it be spoken without effect.
Without the trace of a shadow on it.

Life means all that it ever meant.
It is the same that it ever was.
There is absolute unbroken continuity.
Why should I be out of mind
because I am out of sight?

I am but waiting for you.
For an interval.

Somewhere. Very near.
Just around the corner.

All is well.

Nothing is past; nothing is lost. One brief moment
and all will be as it was before only better, infinitely
happier and forever we will all be one together . . .
Henry Scott Holland

O thou assured soul, thou maidservant of God . . .!
Be not grieved at the death of thy respected husband.
He hath, verily, attained the meeting of his Lord at the
seat of Truth in the presence of the potent King. Do
not suppose that thou hast lost him. The veil shall be
lifted and thou shalt behold his face illumined in the
Supreme Concourse. Just as God, the Exalted, hath
said, 'Him will we surely quicken to a happy life.'
Supreme importance should be attached, therefore,
not to this first creation but rather to the future life.
'Abdu'l-Bahá[5]

As to thy husband, rest assured. He will be immersed
in the ocean of pardon and forgiveness and will
become the recipient of bounty and favour.
'Abdu'l-Bahá[6]

Prayers for Marriage

He is the Bestower, the Bounteous!

Praise be to God, the Ancient, the Ever-Abiding, the Changeless, the Eternal! He Who hath testified in His Own Being that verily He is the One, the Single, the Untrammelled, the Exalted. We bear witness that verily there is no God but Him, acknowledging His oneness, confessing His singleness. He hath ever dwelt in unapproachable heights, in the summits of His loftiness, sanctified from the mention of aught save Himself, free from the description of aught but Him.

And when He desired to manifest grace and beneficence to men, and to set the world in order, He revealed observances and created laws; among them He established the law of marriage, made it as a fortress for well-being and salvation, and enjoined it upon us in that which was sent down out of the heaven of sanctity in His Most Holy Book. He saith, great is His glory: 'Enter into wedlock, O people, that ye may bring forth one who will make mention of Me amid My servants. This is My bidding unto you; hold fast to it as an assistance to yourselves.'

Bahá'u'lláh[1]

He is God!

O peerless Lord! In Thine almighty wisdom Thou hast enjoined marriage upon the peoples, that the generations of men may succeed one another in this

contingent world, and that ever, so long as the world
shall last, they may busy themselves at the Thresh-
old of Thy oneness with servitude and worship, with
salutation, adoration and praise. 'I have not created
spirits and men, but that they should worship me.'
Wherefore, wed Thou in the heaven of Thy mercy
these two birds of the nest of Thy love, and make
them the means of attracting perpetual grace; that
from the union of these two seas of love a wave of
tenderness may surge and cast the pearls of pure and
goodly issue on the shore of life. 'He hath let loose
the two seas, that they meet each other: Between
them is a barrier which they overpass not. Which
then of the bounties of your Lord will ye deny? From
each He bringeth up greater and lesser pearls.'

O Thou kind Lord! Make Thou this marriage to
bring forth coral and pearls. Thou art verily the All-
Powerful, the Most Great, the Ever-Forgiving.

'Abdu'l-Bahá[2]

O my Lord, O my Lord! These two bright orbs are
wedded in Thy love, conjoined in servitude to Thy
Holy Threshold, united in ministering to Thy Cause.
Make Thou this marriage to be as threading lights of
Thine abounding grace, O my Lord, the All-Merci-
ful, and luminous rays of Thy bestowals, O Thou the
Beneficent, the Ever-Giving, that there may branch
out from this great tree boughs that will grow green

and flourishing through the gifts that rain down from Thy clouds of grace.

Verily, Thou art the Generous. Verily, Thou art the Almighty. Verily, Thou art the Compassionate, the All-Merciful.

'Abdu'l-Bahá[3]

With the gentle breeze of Thy compassion, make fresh and green again these boughs, withered by autumn blasts; restore Thou to flourishing life these flowers, shrivelled by the blight of bereavement.

With tidings of the Abhá Paradise, wed Thou our souls to joy, and rejoice Thou our spirits with heartening voices from the dwellers in the realm of glory.

Thou art the Bounteous, Thou art the Clement; Thou art the Bestower, the Loving.

Bahíyyih Khánum[4]

Glory be unto Thee, O my God! Verily, this Thy servant and this Thy maidservant have gathered under the shadow of Thy mercy and they are united through Thy favour and generosity. O Lord! Assist them in this Thy world and Thy kingdom and destine for them every good through Thy bounty and grace. O Lord! Confirm them in Thy servitude and assist them in Thy service. Suffer them to become the signs of Thy Name in Thy world and protect them through Thy bestowals which are inexhaustible in this world and the world to come. O Lord! They are supplicating the kingdom of Thy mercifulness and invoking the realm of Thy singleness. Verily, they are married in obedience to Thy command. Cause them to become the signs of harmony and unity until the end of time. Verily, Thou art the Omnipotent, the Omnipresent and the Almighty!

'Abdu'l-Bahá[5]

I beg of God that thy dear husband be guided through the light of guidance and become a sign of the gift of the Kingdom of Abhá.

'Abdu'l-Bahá[6]

O thou who art advancing unto God!

Verily I pray to God to make thee and thy revered husband – under the shadow of His Greatest Name – confirmed in all conditions, aided in the service of the Cause of God with a confirmation on the part of the Merciful Lord.

O my God! O my God! I ask thee to protect these two birds in the orchard of Thy mercy, confirmed in joy and happiness in the garden of Thy bounties, warbling with the best melodies in the [garden] of Thy knowledge. Verily Thou art the Precious, the Mighty, the Protecting!

'Abdu'l-Bahá[7]

Heavenly Father, send down upon us the dew of your heavenly grace in our married life, that we may have that joy in each other that passes not away, and having lived together in love here, may we ever live together in your glorious kingdom hereafter.

George Hicks

Father, we know that thou art the author of love; that the love which we bear each other is thy gift to us, precious in thy sight, precious in ours. Help us in the years ahead never lightly to regard that gift. We know that the relationship into which we are about to enter is more than moonlight and roses, much more than the singing of love songs and the whispering of our vows of undying affection. We know that in thy sight our marriage will be an eternal union. It is the clasping of our hands, the blending of our lives, the union of our hearts, that we may walk together up the hill of life to meet the dawn, together to bear life's burdens, to discharge its duties, to share its joys and sorrows. We know that our marriage will stand and endure – not by the wedding ceremony or by any marriage licence, but rather by the strength of the love which thou hast given us and by the endurance of our faith in each other and in thee, our Lord, the master of our lives.

And now, as alone with thee we plight this troth: we do promise thee, by thy help, to be faithful and true to each other and to thee who, having given us love and faith in thee, have given us all things.

We thank thee that thy blessing will down the years with us be as a light on our way, as a benediction to the home we are about to establish. May that home always be a haven of strength and love to all who enter it – our neighbours and our friends. We thank thee.

Peter Marshall[8]

With the first light of sun –
Bless you.
When the long day is done – Bless you.
In your smiles and your tears –
Bless you.
Through each day of your years –
Bless you.

Irish wedding blessing

O God of peace, unite our hearts by your bond of peace, that we may live with one another continually in gentleness and humility, in peace and unity. O God of patience in the time of trial, and steadfastness to endure to the end.

Berhard Albrecht

Blessed art though, O Lord, King of the Universe, who created mirth and joy, bridegroom and bride, gladness, jubilation, dancing, and delight, love and brotherhood, peace and fellowship. Quickly, O Lord our God, may the sound of mirth and joy be heard in the streets of Judah and Jerusalem, the voice of bridegroom and bride, jubilant voices of bridegrooms from their canopies and youths from the feasts of song. Blessed art though, O Lord, who makes the bridegroom rejoice with the bride.

Talmud

O Great God! May you grant long life, happiness and health to the ruler of our land, to the community and to the couple.
Grant them all these for many years to enable them to help the worthy.
Give them a long life for many generations.
May there be thousands of blessings upon them.
May the year be happy, the month auspicious and the day propitious.
Grant that for several years, several days, and several months, they may be found worthy and fit to perform religious rites and deeds of charity.
Keep them pure for works of righteousness.
May health, virtue, and goodness be their share.
May it be so.

Zoroastrian marriage blessing

May this couple be blessed with an abundance of resources and comforts, and be helpful to one another in all ways.

May this couple be strong and complement one another.

May this couple be blessed with prosperity and riches on all levels.

May this couple be eternally happy.

May this couple be blessed with a happy family life.

May this couple live in perfect harmony . . . true to their personal values and their joint promises.

May this couple always be the best of friends.

Hindu wedding blessing

O Allah, bless this couple with faith, love and happiness in this world and the next.

Muslim du'a for a wedding

Today we promise to dedicate ourselves completely to each other, with body, speech, and mind.

In this life, in every situation, in wealth or poverty, in health or sickness, in happiness or difficulty, we will work to help each other perfectly.

The purpose of our relationship will be to attain enlightenment by perfecting our kindness and compassion toward all sentient beings.

Lama Thubten Yeshe

Bless them as unmoving and eternal
May their lives flourish like luxuriant trees.
May they, bride and groom, together with heaven
    and earth, with the sun and the moon, continue
    to give out light and radiance.
Thus we do reverently pray.

Shinto wedding blessing

A Talk on Marriage
Attributed to 'Abdu'l-Bahá[1]

The bond that unites hearts most perfectly is loyalty. True lovers once united must show forth the utmost faithfulness one to another. You must dedicate your knowledge, your talents, your fortunes, your titles, your bodies and your spirits to God, to Bahá'u'lláh and to each other. Let your hearts be spacious, as spacious as the universe of God!

Allow no trace of jealousy to creep between you, for jealousy, like unto poison, vitiates the very essence of love. Let not the ephemeral incidents and accidents of this changeful life cause a rift between you. When differences present themselves, take counsel together in secret, lest others magnify a speck into a mountain. Harbour not in your hearts any grievance, but rather explain its nature to each other with such frankness and understanding that it will disappear, leaving no remembrance. Choose fellowship and amity and turn away from jealousy and hypocrisy.

Your thoughts must be lofty, your ideals luminous, your minds spiritual, so that your souls may become a dawning-place for the Sun of Reality. Let your hearts be like two pure mirrors reflecting the stars of the heaven of love and beauty.

Together make mention of noble aspirations and heavenly concepts. Let there be no secrets one from another. Make your house a haven of rest and peace. Be hospitable, and let the doors of your house be open to the faces of friends and strangers. Welcome every guest with radiant grace and let each feel that it is his own home.

No mortal can conceive the union and harmony which God has designed for man and wife. Nourish continually the tree of your union with love and affection, so that it will remain ever green and verdant throughout all seasons and bring forth luscious fruits for the healing of nations.

O beloved of God, may your home be a vision of the paradise of Abhá, so that whosoever enters there may feel the essence of purity and harmony, and cry out from the heart: 'Here is the home of love! Here is the palace of love! Here is the nest of love! Here is the garden of love!'

Be like two sweet-singing birds perched upon the highest branches of the tree of life, filling the air with songs of love and rapture.

Lay the foundation of your affection in the very centre of your spiritual being, at the very heart of your consciousness, and let it not be shaken by adverse winds.

And when God gives you sweet and lovely children, consecrate yourselves to their instruction and guidance, so that they may become imperishable flowers of the divine rose-garden, nightingales of the ideal paradise, servants of the world of humanity, and the fruit of the tree of your life.

Live in such harmony that others may take your lives for an example and may say one to another:

'Look how they live like two doves in one nest, in perfect love, affinity and union. It is as though from all eternity God had kneaded the very essence of their beings for the love of one another.'

Attain the ideal love that God has destined for you, so that you may become partakers of eternal life forthwith. Quaff deeply from the fountain of truth, and dwell all the days of your life in a paradise of glory, gathering immortal flowers from the garden of divine mysteries.

Be to each other as heavenly lovers and divine beloved ones dwelling in a paradise of love. Build your nest on the leafy branches of the tree of love. Soar into the clear atmosphere of love. Sail upon the shoreless sea of love. Walk in the eternal rose-garden of love. Bathe in the shining rays of the sun of love. Be firm and steadfast in the path of love. Perfume your nostrils with the fragrance from the flowers of love. Attune your ears to the soul-entrancing melodies of love. Let your aims be as generous as the banquets of love, and your words as a string of white pearls from the ocean of love. Drink deeply of the elixir of love, so that you may live continually in the reality of Divine Love.

Attributed to 'Abdu'l-Bahá

Joined by God

The Day of God is come. Mankind is approaching maturity. Its spiritual powers and susceptibilities are ripening. It is able at last to understand the true nature of marriage and to make the home what God intended it to be. Holy Writ therefore in this Age gives us pronouncements, counsels, exhortations and commands which call the closest attention of every believer to the sacred institution of marriage and which with all the authority of revelation, assign to it a key-position in the material and spiritual order of human life.

What was taught by precept was confirmed in practice. The Báb, Bahá'u'lláh, and 'Abdu'l-Bahá, the Exemplar of the Faith, were all married men and fathers of families; and the home of 'Abdu'l-Bahá, known to many western visitors, stands as a pattern of what the ideal home of the New Era ought to be.

'Know thou,' wrote 'Abdu'l-Bahá, 'that the command of marriage is eternal. It will never be changed or altered.' True marriage is a spiritual relation between united lovers – a particular state of being to which special blessings are attached by God. 'No mortal can conceive the union and harmony which God has designed for man and wife.' If they are united both spiritually and physically and if the foundation of their affection is laid 'in the very centre of their spiritual being, at the very heart of their consciousness' then they will have 'eternal unity throughout all the divine worlds and improve the spiritual life of each other.' Such union is 'a splendour of the light of the love of God'.

The paying of honour to celibacy as to a condition specially pleasing to God is due to human misunderstanding. In His Tablet to Napoleon III Bahá'u'lláh bade the monks to 'Enter into wedlock that after you another may arise in your stead . . . But for man, who on My earth would remember Me, and how could My attributes and My names be revealed? Reflect and be not of them that have shut themselves out as by a veil from Him, and are of those that are fast asleep.'

Bahá'u'lláh commends marriage, but He does not make entrance into it easy. The initiative lies with the lovers themselves; they are free to choose. But they are strictly enjoined to give to this choice conscientious and deliberate thought. They are to acquire knowledge of each other's character and to make sure beforehand that their outlook on life is in accord on both spiritual and physical matters. They are to be frank and open with each other and if their mutual consent is finally given it is to be complete and entire.

Thus they are expected to employ reason as well as emotion, common sense as well as instinct, in order that they may reach a sound and firm decision; and their union is to represent knowledge as well as love.

When their own consent is given they must obtain before marriage is possible the consent of all their four parents, if living; they must in other words submit their proposed union to the objective judgement of those who know and love them best and who are next to themselves most closely concerned with their happiness. Once this consent is obtained the marriage may go forward.

Thus a Bahá'í marriage is not a personal matter between two united lovers but also a social matter between them and the community and a spiritual matter between them and their heavenly Father. When these relationships are justly combined together, and when as commanded in the Bahá'í revelation the lovers live as equals and can thus help one another to the full limit of their capacity, then is the union real and perfect.

It is not for this earth only. It is intended to be and must be by them regarded as an eternal binding, an everlasting communion and friendship. A true unity of hearts once attained on earth is not dissevered in any of the worlds of God. 'I love thee,' cried the poetess to her husband, 'with the breath, smiles, tears of all my life and if God chooses I shall but love thee better after death.' The fulfilment of this hope is one of the great truths about the eternal realms revealed by Bahá'u'lláh.

The marriage ceremony contains the three elements, the personal, the social, the spiritual. But its unique impressiveness and beauty and power are due to the spiritual meaning which inspires it and the spiritual aspirations which it enshrines. The Bride and the Bridegroom stand before the Bride's man, the Witnesses, and the Bahá'í Reader of their choice; but they stand also in heart and soul before the Mercy-Seat of their Great Father on High. Through their joint declared submission to His will and desire they win the privilege of a sacred union truly made in heaven. From God they seek blessing, happiness and strength for the years to come, and to Him they are directly responsible for the due performance of the precious, divine trust they have undertaken.

How often has 'Abdu'l-Bahá written and spoken of the importance of unity in a home, basing it always on spirituality and telling of the radiance which it sheds afar and of the blessings which it draws down from above. With what power and what exaltation of joy does He in His 'Marriage Tablet'[1] exhort united lovers to this unity! Here indeed is a picture of true marriage – both mystical and practical – which shines with the 'light of the splendour of the love of God'.

He tells lovers how to meet the special tests and strains to which their union may be subjected. 'The bond which unites hearts most perfectly is loyalty,' He writes. 'True lovers once united must show forth the utmost faithfulness one to another.' But He adds at once that they are to dedicate themselves first of all to God and that their hearts are to be 'spacious, as spacious as the universe of God'. He bids them to beware above all of jealousy (which 'vitiates the very essence of love'), of any kind of hypocrisy, of nursing a grievance or making it known to others: rather they are to consult together on their problems in private and to show to one another the greatest frankness and understanding. They are to turn their hearts and their minds towards high, happy, heavenly things and discuss with one another their noblest thoughts and aspirations. Their home is to be 'a haven of rest and peace', for others as well as themselves. 'Be hospitable, and let the doors of your house be open to the faces of friends and strangers. Welcome every guest with radiant grace and let each feel it is his own home.'

They are to be examples of perfect love so that whosoever enters will 'cry out from the heart, "here is the home of love",' and that people will say to one another: 'it is as though from all eternity God had kneaded the very essence of their being for the love of one another'.

Their children are a sacred trust from God to whose instruction and guidance they are to consecrate themselves.

'Abdu'l-Bahá bids them nourish continually their union with love and affection: for it is like a tree, a living, growing, expanding, deepening thing bearing fruits of love and unity that will be 'for the healing of the nations'. In one beautiful image after another He bids them fill their hearts with love, give

themselves up to love, know nothing but love. They
are to dwell in a paradise of love, 'build your nest
in the leafy branches of the tree of love. Soar into
the clear atmosphere of love. Sail upon the shoreless
sea of love. Walk in the eternal rose-garden of love.
Bathe in the shining rays of the sun of love. Be firm
and steadfast in the path of love . . .' In these and all
the other love-laden phrases which He uses He does
more than urge in many forms again and again a
lesson hard enough for imperfect beings to learn and
apply. He reveals in these objective external images
the real existence of a universe of love which only a
lover knows and which only a lover can enter. This
sweeter, fuller life may be a sea on which to sail, a sky
in which to soar, a rose-garden in which to walk, a
sun in whose rays to bathe, a path, a tree, a flower, a
melody, an ocean full of pearls: but always it is a real
world created for lovers, offered to lovers, laid open
for their use, a world of unshadowed beauty and infi-
nite delight wherein they may go forward together
passing from discovery to discovery, from happiness
to further happiness.

If this world be hidden from men it is hidden in
the heart of Truth and the veil that blinds unloving
eyes is the veil of inexperience and ignorance. It is,
as He shows, of the essence of existence. If the lover
sees his beloved transform for him the living earth
around him, this is not an idle dream:

Yours is not a conscious art;
'Tis the wild magic of your heart.
You but speak a simple word,
Often said and often heard,
When before my wondering eyes
An unveiléd Paradise
Bursts about me into flower.
Here each nimble-footed hour
Daft with all the fun that's in it
Dances like a madcap minute.
All the earth in light unfolden
Seems a chamber green and golden
Dight for love's festivities;
And a thousand harmonies,
Softer, sweeter more endeared
Than my heart had ever heard,
Gush from every bank and rise
Fill the woods and touch the skies.
Wind and cloud and leaf and stream
Notes of purest music seem,
And all nature, like a choir
Tunúd to the sun-god's lyre,
In new hymns of jubilee
Chants her ancient ecstasy.

Love is the true revealer and the passage of time takes nothing from such a vision. United lovers who through all the years have fought side by side the rugged battle of life unyielding, who have shared anxiety and trial and sorrow, who have mingled their tears together – tears of grief as well as tears of joy, who have seen one another falter and stumble and go on again, who have helped and been helped, have forgiven and been forgiven, they know as none other can know how precious is fellowship in love, and with a fuller illumination and a deeper thankfulness than of old they say again the sacred verse that made them forever one: 'We are content with the will of God; we are satisfied with the desire of God.'[2]

'Abdu'l-Bahá was the Exemplar of the perfect life, and to His word God gave creative power. This Tablet of His is itself a Marriage Song so exalted, so joyous, so triumphant, aglow in every part with overflowing, outpouring, illimitable, heavenly love that it makes love seem the Reality, the Essence of all existence, and puts all unlovingness to shame.

George Townshend[3]

Bibliography

'Abdu'l-Bahá. *Paris Talks*. London: Bahá'í Publishing Trust, 1995.

— *The Promulgation of Universal Peace*. Wilmette, IL: Bahá'í Publishing Trust, 1982.

— *Selections from the Writings of 'Abdu'l-Bahá*. Haifa: Bahá'í World Centre, 1978.

— *Tablets of Abdul-Baha Abbas*. Chicago: Bahá'í Publishing Society; vol. 1, 1909; vol. 2, 1915; vol. 3, 1916.

Abdul Baha on Divine Philosophy. Boston: The Tudor Press, 1918.

'Abdu'l-Bahá in London. London: Bahá'í Publishing Trust, 1987.

Aristotle. *Politics*. Various editions.

The Báb. *Selections from the Writings of the Báb*. Haifa: Bahá'í World Centre, 1976.

The Baháʼí Faith: The Website of the Worldwide Baháʼí Community. https://www.bahai.org/

Baháʼí International Community, *The Family in a World Community.* Pamphlet first distributed at the World NGO Forum Launching the United Nations International Year of the Family (IYF). Malta, 25 November 1993.

Baháʼí Prayers. https://www.bahai.org/library/authoritative-texts/prayers/bahai-prayers/1#346585691

— https://www.bahai.org/library/authoritative-texts/prayers/bahai-prayers/3#054499841

— https://www.bahai.org/library/authoritative-texts/prayers/bahai-prayers/3#279311388

— https://www.bahai.org/library/authoritative-texts/prayers/bahai-prayers/3#287304205

— https://www.bahai.org/library/authoritative-texts/prayers/bahai-prayers/3#301244991

The Baháʼí World. vols. 1–12, 1925–54. rpt. Wilmette, IL: Baháʼí Publishing Trust, 1980.

Baháʼí World Faith. Wilmette, IL: Baháʼí Publishing Trust, 2nd ed. 1976.

Baháʼuʼlláh. *The Kitáb-i-Aqdas.* Haifa: Baháʼí World Centre, 1992.

— *Prayers and Meditations.* Wilmette, IL: Baháʼí Publishing Trust, 1987.

— 'Seven Valleys', *Call of the Divine Beloved: Selected Mystical Works of Bahá'u'lláh*. 2019.

https://www.bahai.org/library/authoritativetexts/bahaullah/calldivinebeloved/calldivinebeloved.pdf?92cc9eb5

— *Tablets of Bahá'u'lláh*. Wilmette, IL: Bahá'í Publishing Trust, 1988.

Bahíyyih Khánum, the Greatest Holy Leaf: A Compilation from Bahá'í Sacred Texts and Writings of the Guardian of the Faith and Bahíyyih Khánum's Own Letters. Haifa: Bahá'í World Centre, 1982.

Bennett, W. C. *The Worn Wedding-Ring, and Other Poems*. London: Chapman and Hall, 1861.

de Bernieres, Louis. *Captain Corelli's Mandolin*. London: Secker &Warburg, 1994.

The Bible. New International Version (NIV). Various editions,

The Bible. New King James Version (NKJV). Various editions.

A Book of Prayers for the First Years of Marriage. Oxford: Lion Publishing, 1995.

Carnegie, Dale. *How to Stop Worrying and Start Living*. La Vergne, TN: BN Publishing, 2011.

The Compilation of Compilations. Prepared by the Universal House of Justice 1963–1990. 2 vols. [Mona Vale NSW]: Bahá'í Publications Australia, 1991.

Family Life. Compiled by the Research Department of the Universal House of Justice. Haifa: Bahá'í World Centre, 1982.

For Your Marriage. Part of the National Pastoral Initiative for Marriage, an initiative of the United States Conference of Catholic Bishops. http://www.foryourmarriage.org/meaning-and-purpose/

Fowers, Blaine J., Ph.D. *Beyond the Myth of Marital Happiness*. San Francisco: Jossey-Bass, 2000.

'From the Diary of Mirza Ahmad Sohrab', 7 January 1914, in 'Abdul-Baha on Spiritual Happiness', *Star of the West*, vol. 7, no. 9, p. 81.

Frost, Robert. 'The Death of the Hired Man', in *North of Boston*. London: David Nutt, 1914.

Hugo, Victor. *Les Misérables*. London: Penguin Classics, 1982.

Ives, Howard Colby. *Portals to Freedom*. Oxford: George Ronald, 1973.

Keller, Timothy J. and Keller, Kathy. *The Meaning of Marriage: Facing the Complexities of Commitment with the Wisdom of God*. New York: Dutton Adult, 2011.

à Kempis, Thomas. 'The Imitation of Christ'. Various editions.

Lights of Guidance: A Bahá'í Reference File. Compiled by Helen Hornby. New Delhi: Bahá'í Publishing Trust, 3rd ed. 1994.

Love, Pat. *The Truth About Love: The Highs, the Lows, and How You Can Make It Last Forever*. New York: Touchstone, 2001.

The Lovers' Dictionary: A Poetical Treasury of Lovers' Thoughts, Fancies, Addresses, and Dilemmas. New York: Harper & Brothers, 1867.

Marriage Transformation. https://marriagetransformation.com/

Munírih Khánum: Memoirs and Letters. trans. Sammireh Anwar Smith. Los Angeles: Kalimát Press, 1987.

Parrott, Les and Leslie Parrott. *Becoming Soul Mates*. Grand Rapids, MI: Zondervan. 1995.

Paul, Dr Robert S. *Finding Ever After: A Romantic Adventure for Her, An Adventurous Romance for Him*. Bloomington, MN: Bethany House, 2007.

Peck, M. Scott. *The Road Less Travelled*. London: Arrow New-Age, new ed. 1990.

Rabbaní, Rúhíyyih. *Prescription for Living*. London: George Ronald, rev. ed. 1960.

— *The Priceless Pearl*. London: Bahá'í Publishing Trust, 1969.

Ruhe, Margaret. *Some Thoughts on Marriage*. Los Angeles: Kalimát Press, 1982.

Rumi, Jalalu'd-Din. *Mathnavi*. Various editions.

Service of the Heart. Jewish tradition. Various editions.

Shoghi Effendi. *Dawn of a New Day: Messages to India 1923-1957*. New Delhi: Bahá'í Publishing Trust, 1970.

— Letter to an individual, 15 July 1928.

— Letter written on behalf of Shoghi Effendi
  — to an individual, 27 April 1926.
  — to an individual, 14 May 1929.
  — to an individual, 13 November 1931.
  — to an individual, 6 November 1932.
  — to the National Spiritual Assembly of India, 6 July 1935.
  — to an individual, 8 May 1939.
  — to an individual in India, 16 November 1939.
  — 16 December 1940.
  — to an individual, 28 September 1941.
  — to an individual, 20 January 1943.
  — to an individual, 4 August 1943.
  — to an individual, 16 March 1946.
  — to the National Spiritual Assembly of the United States and Canada, 25 October 1947.
  — to an individual, 3 November 1947.
  — to an individual, 5 April 1952.
  — 6 July 1952.
  — to an individual, 12 July 1952.
  — to an individual, 3 March 1955.
  — 6 September 1956.
  — to a National Spiritual Assembly, 9 November 1956.

— *The Unfolding Destiny of the British Bahá'í Community: The Messages of the Guardian of the Bahá'í Faith to the Bahá'ís of the British Isles*. London: Bahá'í Publishing Trust, 1981.

Star of the West. rpt., vols. 7, 11. Oxford: George Ronald, 1984.

Stevenson, Robert Louis. 'Songs of Travel' (1895), in *Poems, including Underwoods, Ballads, Songs of Travel*. London: Chatto & Windus, 1917.

Townshend, George. 'Joined by God', in *Bahá'í World*, vol. 9, p. 744.

— *The Mission of Bahá'u'lláh and Other Literary Pieces*. London: George Ronald, 1965.

The Universal House of Justice. 'An unauthenticated record by Ahmad Sohrab of a talk by 'Abdu'l-Bahá', in *American Bahá'í*, September 1992.

— Letter of the Universal House of Justice

  — to the National Spiritual Assembly of South and West Africa, 18 January 1971.

  — to an individual, 24 January 1993.

— Letter written on behalf of the Universal House of Justice

  — 1 August 1978.

  — to an individual, 8 May 1979.

  — to individuals, 24 June 1979.

  — 17 July 1979.

  — to a National Spiritual Assembly, 28 December 1980.

— 16 May 1982.

— 2 November 1982.

— to an individual, 25 July 1984.

— to an individual, 30 August 1984.

— to an individual, 23 July 1985.

— to an individual, 27 October 1986.

— to an individual, 2 January 1990.

— 24 January 1993.

— Message to the Oceanic Conference, Palermo, Sicily, August 1968.

— Message written on behalf of the Universal House of Justice to the European Bahá'í Youth Council, 7 December 1992.

— *Messages from the Universal House of Justice 1968–1973.* Wilmette, IL: Bahá'í Publishing Trust, 1976.

Wells, J.M. *From the Sublime to the Ridiculous: Poems from the Land of the First Light,* unpublished ms.

Wilmette Institute. http://wilmetteinstitute.org/

Yaconelli, Michael. *Dangerous Wonder: The Adventure of Childlike Faith.* Carol Stream, IL: Navpress, 2003.

Zoroaster, Avesta, *Vahishto-Ishti Gatha Yasna.* Various editions.

References

Preface

1. From a letter written on behalf of Shoghi Effendi to the National Spiritual Assembly of India, 6 July 1935.

2. Bahá'í International Community, *Family in a World Community.*

Meaning and Purpose of Marriage

1. 'Abdu'l-Bahá, *Selections*, p. 118.

2. 'Abdu'l-Bahá, *Selections*, p. 120.

3. From a letter written on behalf of Shoghi Effendi, 17 February 1940.

4. From a letter written on behalf of Shoghi Effendi to an individual, 15 April 1939.

5. Shoghi Effendi, quoted in a letter of the Universal House of Justice to an individual, 31 July 1970.

6. From a letter written on behalf of Shoghi Effendi to an individual, 14 October 1935.

7. For Your Marriage, part of the National Pastoral Initiative for Marriage, an initiative of the United States Conference of Catholic Bishops: http://www.foryourmarriage.org/meaning-and-purpose/

Sanctity of Marriage

1. From a letter written on behalf of Shoghi Effendi, 10 August 1945.

2. From a letter written on behalf of Shoghi Effendi, 17 October 1944.

3. From a letter written on behalf of Shoghi Effendi, 5 April 1951.

4. From a letter written on behalf of Shoghi Effendi, 10 November 1943.

5. From a letter written on behalf of the Universal House of Justice, 3 November 1982.

Love

1. 'Abdu'l-Bahá, *Paris Talks*, p. 139.

2. Rabbaní, Prescription for Living, p. 62.

3. 'Abdu'l-Bahá, *Paris Talks*, pp. 179–81.

4. Thomas à Kempis, from 'The Imitation of Christ'.

5. 'Abdu'l-Bahá, *Selections*, pp. 27–8.

6. Bahá'u'lláh, 'Seven Valleys', *Call of the Divine Beloved*, https://www.bahai.org/library/authoritative-texts/bahau llah/call-divine-beloved/call-divine-beloved.pdf?80c576fd

7. Bahá'u'lláh, 'Seven Valleys'.

8. *Sanáʼí*, quoted by Bahá'u'lláh, in 'Seven Valleys'.

9. Jalalu'd-Din Rumi, from *Mathnavi*, quoted by Bahá'u'lláh in 'Seven Valleys'.

10. Recounted by Bahá'u'lláh, in 'Seven Valleys'.

11. Louis de Bernieres, from *Captain Corelli's Mandolin*.

12. Bahá'u'lláh, 'Seven Valleys'.

13. Keller, *Meaning of Marriage*.

14. Wells, *From the Sublime to the Ridiculous: Poems from the Land of the First Light*, unpublished ms.

15. Hugo, from *Les Misérables*.

The Path to Marriage

1. 'Abdu'l-Bahá, in *Bahá'í World Faith*, p. 372.

2. 'Abdu'l-Bahá, from a talk given on 22 December 1918 in

Haifa; in *Star of the West*, vol. 11, no. 1, 21 March 1920.

3. From a letter written on behalf of the Universal House of Justice, 17 July 1979.

4. From a letter of the Universal House of Justice, 2 November 1982.

5. Written on behalf of the Universal House of Justice to an individual, 27 October 1986.

6. From a letter written on behalf of Shoghi Effendi to an individual, 20 January 1943.

7. Robert Louis Stevenson, *Songs of Travel*.

8. From a letter written on behalf of Shoghi Effendi to an individual, 17 January 1939, in *Compilation*, vol. 2, p. 446.

Engagement

1. 'Abdu'l-Bahá, *Selections*, p. 118.

2. From a letter written on behalf of Shoghi Effendi to the National Spiritual Assembly of the United States and Canada, 25 October 1947.

3. 'Abdu'l-Bahá, *Selections*, p. 118.

4. From a letter of Universal House of Justice to an individual, 24 January 1993.

5. From a letter written on behalf of Shoghi Effendi.

The Wedding

1. 'Abdu'l-Bahá, in *Abdu'l-Baha in London*, pp. 78–9.

2. 'Abdu'l-Bahá, *Selections*, p. 119.

3. Munírih <u>Kh</u>ánum, *Memoirs and Letters*, pp. 46–51.

4. Rúḥíyyih Rabbaní, *Priceless Pearl*, pp. 151–2.

5. Bahá'u'lláh, *Kitáb-i-Aqdas*, p. 105.

A Marriage of Love

1. 'Abdu'l-Bahá, *Selections*, p. 117.
2. From a letter written on behalf of Shoghi Effendi, 20 January 1943.
3. Bahá'í Prayers. https://www.bahai.org/library/authoritative -texts/prayers/bahai-prayers/3#054499841
4. 'Abdu'l-Bahá, in *Bahá'í World Faith*, p. 229.

A Marriage of Unity

1. From a letter written on behalf of Shoghi Effendi to a National Spiritual Assembly, 9 November 1956.
2. Keller, *Meaning of Marriage*.
3. From a letter written on behalf of Shoghi Effendi, 6 September 1956.
4. From a letter written on behalf of the Universal House of Justice, 1 August 1978.
5. 'Abdu'l-Bahá, *Selections*, p. 119.
6. Bahá'í International Community, *Family in a World Community*.
7. 'Abdu'l-Bahá, *Selections*, p. 279.

Dimensions of a Spiritual Marriage

1. 'Abdu'l-Bahá, *Selections*, p. 117.
2. From letter written on behalf of Shoghi Effendi to an individual, 8 May 1939.
3. Keller, *The Meaning of Marriage*.
4. 'Abdu'l-Bahá, *Selections*, p. 122.
5. 'Abdu'l-Bahá, *Tablets*, vol. 2, p. 325.
6. From a letter written on behalf of Shoghi Effendi to an individual, 28 September 1941.
7. Bahá'u'lláh, in 'Women', *Compilation*, vol. 2, p. 379.

8. 'Abdu'l-Bahá, *Promulgation*, p. 182.

9. 'Abdu'l-Bahá, *Selections*, pp. 79–80.

10. Fowers, *Beyond the Myth of Marital Happiness*, p. 185.

11. Love, *The Truth About Love*, p. 132.

12. From a letter written on behalf of Shoghi Effendi to an individual, 4 August 1943.

13. Parrott, *Becoming Soul Mates*, p. 20.

14. From a message written on behalf of the Universal House of Justice to the European Bahá'í Youth Council, 7 December 1992.

15. From a letter written on behalf of Shoghi Effendi to an individual, 12 July 1952.

16. From a letter written on behalf of Shoghi Effendi to an individual, 3 March 1955.

17. 'Abdu'l-Bahá, *Paris Talks*, p. 162.

18. Zoroaster, Avesta, *Vahishto-Ishti Gatha Yasna* 53, 5.

19. 'Abdu'l-Bahá, *Promulgation*, p. 469.

20. 'Abdu'l-Bahá, *Promulgation*, p. 453.

21. 'Abdu'l-Bahá, *Selections*, p. 118.

22. Ruhe, *Some Thoughts on Marriage*, p. 4.

23. Love, *The Truth About Love*, p. 150.

Creating a Strong Marriage

1. 'Abdu'l-Bahá, *Selections*, pp. 229–30.

2. Keller, *Meaning of Marriage*.

3. Rabbaní, *Prescription for Living*, p. 65.

4. 'Abdu'l-Bahá, in *Bahá'í World Faith*, p. 368.

5. 'Abdu'l-Bahá, *Paris Talks*, p. 17.

6. 'Abdu'l-Bahá, *Bahá'í World Faith*, p. 429.

7. Bahá'u'lláh, *Tablets*, p. 168.

8. Bahá'u'lláh, in *Compilation*, vol. 1, p. 93.

9. 'Abdu'l-Bahá, *Promulgation*, p. 183.

10. 'Abdu'l-Bahá, *Selections*, pp. 128–9.

11. Bahá'u'lláh, in *Compilation*, vol. 1, p. 93.

12. From a letter written on behalf of the Universal House of Justice to an individual, 2 January 1990.

13. 'Abdu'l-Bahá, in *Compilation*, vol. 1, p. 97.

14. From a letter written on behalf of the Universal House of Justice to a National Spiritual Assembly, 28 December 1980.

15. From a letter written on behalf of the Universal House of Justice, 16 May 1982.

16. From a letter written on behalf of the Universal House of Justice, 24 January 1993.

A Home Together

1. Bahá'í Prayers. https://www.bahai.org/library/authoritative-texts/prayers/bahai-prayers/1#346585691

2. Bahá'u'lláh, in *Compilation*, vol. 2, pp. 385–6.

3. Bahá'u'lláh, *Kitáb-i-Aqdas*, para. 108.

4. *Star of the West*, vol. 9, no. 3, p. 40.

5. From a letter written on behalf of Shoghi Effendi to an individual, 13 November 1931.

6. 'Abdu'l-Bahá, in *Compilation*, vol. 2, p. 340.

7. 'Abdu'l-Bahá, quoted in a letter written on behalf of the Universal House of Justice to an individual, 30 August 1984.

8. 'Abdu'l-Bahá, *Compilation*, vol. 2, p. 392.

9. The Báb, *Selections*, p. 200.

10. 'Abdu'l-Bahá, *Tablets*, vol. 1, p. 69.

11. Townshend, *Mission of Bahá'u'lláh*, p. 147.

12. ibid. p. 148.

13. Bahá'u'lláh, *Prayers and Meditations*, pp. 126–7.

14. Frost, 'The Death of the Hired Man'.

15. Bahá'u'lláh, *Prayers and Meditations*, pp. 257–8.

16. ibid. p. 266.

17. The Báb, *Selections*, p. 193.

18. 'An unauthenticated record by Ahmad Sohrab of a talk by 'Abdu'l-Bahá', in The Universal House of Justice, *American Bahá'í*, September 1992.

19. 'Abdu'l-Bahá, *Selections*, p. 195.

20. 'Abdu'l-Bahá, *Tablets*, vol. 1, pp. 68–9.

21. 'Abdu'l-Bahá, *Promulgation*, p. 4.

22. 'Abdu'l-Bahá, *Tablets*, vol. 3, pp. 665–6.

23. 'Abdu'l-Bahá, *Promulgation*, p. 75.

24. From a talk of 'Abdu'l-Bahá, in *Family Life*, p. 219.

25. From letter written on behalf of Shoghi Effendi to an individual, 6 November 1932.

26. From a letter written on behalf of Shoghi Effendi to an individual in India, 16 November 1939, in *Dawn of a New Day*, p. 202.

27. From letter written on behalf of Shoghi Effendi to an individual, 14 May 1929.

28. From letter written on behalf of Shoghi Effendi to an individual, 16 March 1946.

29. From a letter written on behalf of Shoghi Effendi, 6 July 1952.

30. From letter written on behalf of Shoghi Effendi to an individual, 27 April 1926.

Becoming a Family

1. 'Abdu'l-Bahá, *Tablets*, vol. 3, pp. 605–6.

2. 'Abdu'l-Bahá, *Tablets*, vol. 2, p. 262.

3. 'Abdu'l-Bahá, *Abdu'l-Baha in London*, p. 111.

4. 'Abdu'l-Bahá, *Tablets*, vol. 3, p. 606.
5. Bahá'u'lláh, in *Compilation*, vol. 1, pp. 1–2.
6. 'Abdu'l-Bahá, 'Talk at Children's Meeting, Hotel Plaza, Chicago, Illinois', 5 May 1912, in *Promulgation*, pp. 91–2.
7. Townshend, *Mission of Bahá'u'lláh*, p. 147.
8. 'Abdu'l-Bahá, in *Bahá'í World Faith*, p. 229.
9. 'Abdu'l-Bahá, in *Divine Philosophy*, p. 183.
10. 'Abdu'l-Bahá, *Promulgation*, p. 168.
11. Peck, *Road Less Travelled*, p. 159.
12. From a letter written on behalf of the Universal House of Justice to an individual, 25 July 1984.
13. 'Abdu'l-Bahá, *Selections*, p. 279.
14. 'Abdu'l-Bahá, *Tablets*, vol. 1, p. 59.
15. 'Abdu'l-Bahá, *Tablets*, vol. 2, p. 252.
16. 'Abdu'l-Bahá, *Tablets*, vol. 3, p. 527.

A Marriage of Joy, Play and Laughter

1. 'Abdu'l-Bahá, in *Bahá'í World Faith*, p. 360.
2. 'Abdu'l-Bahá, *Paris Talks*, p. 165.
3. Attributed to 'Abdu'l-Bahá, in 'From the Diary of Mirza Ahmad Sohrab', 7 January 1914, in 'Abdul-Baha on Spiritual Happiness', *Star of the West*, vol. 7, no. 9, p. 81.
4. 'Abdu'l-Bahá, in *Bahá'í World Faith*, p. 365.
5. 'Abdu'l-Bahá, *Tablets*, vol. 2, p. 320.
6. Rumi, *Mathnavi*, quoted in 'Seven Valleys'. https://www.bahai.org/library/authoritative-texts/bahaullah/call-divine-beloved/call-divine-beloved.pdf?5f4cfff8
7. 'Abdu'l-Bahá, in *Bahá'í World Faith*, p. 353.
8. Bahá'u'lláh, *Kitáb-i-Aqdas*, para. 156.
9. Shoghi Effendi, in *Unfolding Destiny*, p. 457.
10. The Universal House of Justice, Message to the Oceanic Conference, Palermo, Sicily, August 1968.

11. From a letter written on behalf of Shoghi Effendi to an individual, 3 November 1947.

12. Dale Carnegie, *How to Stop Worrying and Start Living*, p. 24.

13. Aristotle, *Politics* 1339b (15, 20).

14. Michael Yaconelli, *Dangerous Wonder*, pp. 78–9.

15. Dr Robert S. Paul, *Finding Ever After*, p. 233.

16. ibid. pp. 235–6.

17. Ives, *Portals to Freedom*, pp. 117–20.

18. 'Abdu'l-Bahá, *Promulgation*, p. 218.

19. 'Abdu'l-Bahá, in *Star of the West*, vol. 7, p. 101.

20. 'Abdu'l-Bahá, *Selections*, p. 236.

21. From a letter written on behalf of the Universal House of Justice to an individual, 23 July 1985.

22. Rumi, *Mathnavi*, quoted in 'Seven Valleys'. https://www.bahai.org/library/authoritative-texts/bahaullah/call-divine-beloved/call-divine-beloved.pdf?5f4cfff8

23. From a letter written on behalf of the Universal House of Justice to an individual, 8 May 1979.

In Times of Difficulty

1. 'Abdu'l-Bahá, *Tablets*, vol. 1, p. 98.

2. From a letter written on behalf of the Universal House of Justice, 17 July 1979.

3. From a letter written on behalf of Shoghi Effendi to an individual, 5 April 1952.

4. 'Abdu'l-Bahá, *Bahá'í World Faith*, p. 386.

5. 'Abdu'l-Bahá, *Tablets*, vol. 1, p. 91.

6. From a letter written on behalf of Shoghi Effendi to an individual, 15 July 1928.

7. From a letter written on behalf of the Universal House of Justice to an individual, 24 June 1979.

8. From a letter written on behalf of Shoghi Effendi to an individual, 23 July 1937.

Marriage Through Life's Stages

1. From letter written on behalf of Shoghi Effendi to an individual, 6 November 1932.

2. From a letter written on behalf of Shoghi Effendi to an individual, 13 December 1940.

3. 'Abdu'l-Bahá, in *Abdu'l-Baha in London*, pp. 78–9.

4. From a talk of 'Abdu'l-Bahá, in *Family Life*, p. 219.

5. From a letter written on behalf of Shoghi Effendi, 16 December 1940.

Together Forever

1. From a Tablet of 'Abdu'l-Bahá, in 'Give Me Thy Grace to Serve Thy Loved Ones'. http://bahai-library.com/pdf/compilations/compilation_serve_loved_ones.pdf

2. 'Abdu'l-Bahá, *Selections*, p. 118.

3. 'Abdu'l-Bahá, *Abdu'l-Baha in London*, p. 96.

4. 'Abdu'l-Bahá, *Abdu'l-Baha in London*, p. 75.

5. 'Abdu'l-Bahá, *Selections*, p. 197.

6. 'Abdu'l-Bahá, *Selections*, p. 200.

Prayers for Marriage

1. Bahá'í Prayers. https://www.bahai.org/library/authoritative-texts/prayers/bahai-prayers/3#279311388

2. Bahá'í Prayers. https://www.bahai.org/library/authoritative-texts/prayers/bahai-prayers/3#054499841

3. Bahá'í Prayers. https://www.bahai.org/library/authoritative-texts/prayers/bahai-prayers/3#287304205

4. Bahíyyih Khánum, in *Bahíyyih Khánum*, p. 150.

5. Bahá'í Prayers. https://www.bahai.org/library/authoritative
   -texts/prayers/bahai-prayers/3#301244991
6. 'Abdu'l-Bahá, *Tablets*, vol. 3, p. 689.
7. 'Abdu'l-Bahá, *Tablets*, vol. 1, p. 48.
8. Marshall, in *Book of Prayers for the First Years of Marriage*.

A Talk on Marriage Attributed to 'Abdu'l-Bahá

1. 'With regard to your question concerning the so-called Marriage Tablet printed on page 47 of the supplement of the British Prayer Book, this is not a Tablet, but a talk ascribed to the Master by Mírzá Ahmad Sohrab. It was given some time in December, 1918 about Sohrab's marriage. It cannot be regarded as Bahá'í scripture as "nothing can be considered as scripture for which we do not have an original text", as the beloved Guardian pointed out. The friends may use this talk, but it is not to be considered as scripture.' From a letter of the Universal House of Justice to the National Spiritual Assembly of South and West Africa, 18 January 1971.

Joined by God

1. As mentioned above, the 'Marriage Tablet' is a talk given by 'Abdu'l-Bahá. Bahá'ís 'may use this talk, but it is not to be considered as scripture.' See endnote 1 of chapter 18.
2. The authoritative translation of both passages is, 'We will all, verily, abide by the Will of God.' Bahá'u'lláh, *Kitáb-i-Aqdas*, p. 105.
3. Townshend, 'Joined by God', *Bahá'í World*, vol. 9, pp. 741–5.